IRA TAC

IRA
TACTICS
&TARGETS

J. Bowyer Bell

POOLBEG

First published 1990 by
Poolbeg Press Ltd
Knocksedan House,
Swords, Co Dublin, Ireland

© J. Bowyer Bell 1990
Reprinted 1993

ISBN 1 85371 257 4

All rights reserved. No part of this publication may be reproduced or transmitted in any form or by any means, electronic or mechanical, including photography, recording, or any information storage or retrieval system, without permission in writing from the publisher. The book is sold subject to the condition that it shall not, by way of trade or otherwise, be lent, resold or otherwise circulated without the publisher's prior consent in any form of binding or cover other than that in which it is published and without a similar condition including this condition being imposed on the subsequent purchaser.

Cover design by Pomphrey Associates
Typeset by Print-Forme
Printed by Cox & Wyman Ltd,
Reading, Berks

Contents

	page
Foreword	i
Introduction	1
The Irish Republican Army	8
Ideology	9
The Organization	11
Strategy	17
Tactics	19
Republican Alternatives	20
The Dynamic of IRA Strategy and Tactics	26
IRA Targets	
People	29
Places	38
IRA Targets: Case Studies	55

The Individual as Target: Categories and Symbols	59
Sniping Ambush, Derry City, March 1972	61
Assassination Attempt on General Sir Ian Freeland, Summer 1971	65
Assassination Attempt on John Taylor MP, February 25, 1972	68
Assassination of Ambassador Christopher Ewart-Biggs, July 21, 1976	71
Assassination of Lord Mountbatten, August 27, 1979	73
Assassination of Seamus Costello, October 1977	77
Resources as Target: Destruction and Acquisition	82
Derry Car-bombs, March 21, 1972	83
Bloody Friday, Belfast, July 21, 1972	85
The Dublin-Belfast Railway Link	89
The Great Train Robbery	92
Review	
Structure and Conceptions	104
The IRA Center	109
In Sum	114
The Sources	117

Foreword

After a generation the IRA armed struggle, often spectacular, is consistently lethal, and rarely disappears from public concern. Even for those with no Irish connections, even for those thousands of miles away, even for those on the scene who discount the low level of real violence the Troubles are hard news. This news is interpreted first by the perceptions of those involved, then by the media acting as conduit for dramatic tidings and is finally adjusted by the various observers. There is little consensus, many competing truths, no agreed reality. After all this time there remain those who imagine the IRA, a major player in the present Irish game, as a conglomerate of the mad acting without reason or logic, bloody-minded addicts of violence. After the IRA bomb at Deal, Kent, that killed ten military bandsmen on September 22, 1989, Prince Charles wondered "...what sort of mentality can contemplate such meaningless acts. It is appalling." There are others who see the IRA as a creature of wicked, evil men not crazed but malevolent, a creature of the Roman Catholic Church, a creature of international communism eager to establish a new Cuba, a creature of some other useful fantasy. And for others the Republican volunteers are without fault, patriots all, above reproach, skilled, competent guerrillas seeking only a nation once again. But few would accept the IRA as knights-errant, even those who still imagine a united Ireland. Certainly, even the calm and judicious, those neither threatened by the IRA campaign nor in a position to benefit by the outcome, are often at a loss to discern logic, even self-interest, in the Provisional IRA's actions. There appear to have been those in the IRA without a firm grip on reality—or is this hapless record intended? Advocates of non-violence, diplomacy, tact and compromise, parliamentary politics or the easy life—most people—find IRA actions unpalatable, often inexplicable. What do they intend? What do they seek to gain?

In general, the IRA does not care about the priorities of others, dances to its own tune, performs for a different constituency, not all among the living, and so plays by history's rules as read by generations of the faithful. Direction of an armed struggle is no easy matter. Mistakes are inevitable. Yet in the end history rules, justice as defined by the patriot dead and the present volunteers will win, as has been the case before. These rules are not to be read from an open book but are at least rational and not unreasonable in intent and prospect. The IRA campaign in reality has a logic and a direction amenable to analysis. Even a secret army cannot after a generation make a full secret of means and methods, goals and targets—not if they are, as has been the case over the years, willing to discuss such matters with those only visiting their covert world. Thus this is a brief foray into the nature of IRA targets and tactics, into the center of the circle where most matters of strategy and tactics are seldom discussed, where consensus does reign and history's rules are accepted as given. The particulars of analysis have been selected from the available examples but rest on endless discussions concerning all aspects of the Republican movement for a generation. Some operations remain secret because of the vulnerabilities of those involved, some because there are no longer witnesses available. Obviously the more detailed cases tend to be more public, more amenable to analysis, but a few are included simply because I was there as witness. Proximity may to a degree contaminate, but which historian would refuse an opportunity to watch Waterloo or Easter Week? Still, the foundation of this analytical effort remains those involved, rather than more conventional historical sources or even the written word.

JBB

Dublin and New York, 1990

Introduction

In theory, if not always in practice, one of the enormous assets of a secret army is secrecy. On one side looms the authorized power of the state, blocks of soldiers, armor at the corner, hourly news broadcasts, hospitals and a bureaucracy, ambassadors at the United Nations and police at the front door. On the other side there is nothing or nothing much visible, a few posters, scrawled slogans, perhaps a closely monitored legal party, perhaps not. Mostly nothing. The authorities often suspect much, have lists and diagrams, often computers filled with names or drawers with files on suspects; but even then little of the dynamics of the other side, the underground, is really understood by the conventional. And for that matter, little time can be allotted by those underground to such analysis, to internal dissection; for simply to persist in the armed struggle requires all the available assets. So secret armies often stay secret, even to those enlisted, who rarely know anything but bits and pieces, just their proper role, all that is necessary, often too much as it is. In time such revolutionary organizations may have a historian; but in the midst of the campaign, there is neither time nor place for detailed analysis, an exercise that may not help those already stretched thin by the demands of an unconventional, low-intensity war.

For the conventional one of the more unorthodox aspects of any such low-intensity conflict has always been the unexpected, the quite unforeseen strike by the covert irregulars producing surprise, dismay, indignation, and frustration. The secret armies, the assassins, the terrorists always, always, seem to have the capacity to produce, on demand, in their own time, the unconventional. And they continue to do so no matter how painstaking the preparations, how thoroughly the threatened parse past history and present practice: every time deceived, dismayed, every time unprepared. In a long campaign, an irregular war paralleling the orthodox, a war of ambush in the outback or a rural guerrilla campaign, this asymmetrical, violent dialogue gradually evolves patterns and rules for the conventional, the conventions of unconventional war. These, then, can be taught in the academy and deployed in the field. As low-intensity war moves into the cities, into the more advanced societies, these anti-insurgency tactics, even when adjusted for the new arena, may restrict the rebels' options but rarely their capacity to strike against targets, seemingly when and where they choose, and often by a means quite unforeseen.

These sudden, unanticipated strikes out of the underground by a secret army as much as any aspect of a low-intensity conflict make unconventional war unconventional. Cunningly planned, brutal, spectacular and always a surprise, such operations may have enormous impact on the course of events even when they do not return real power to the rebels. In some cases insurgents seek prominence as much as power or symbolic gain or even vengeance publicly displayed. Such terrorists seem the most unconventional rebels of all, as they choreograph atrocity. For our era the very words Munich, Moro, and Mountbatten evoke an age of horrors, a time of almost inexplicable terror, a threat without appropriate response.

Terror is no more inexplicable than any other rationally chosen strategy of conflict, a necessary means to an end, not the conduct of the mad and rarely the act of a mercenary. Even alien volunteers are more often bought with a slogan than on the hire-purchase. Terrorists, like rebels, are believers, usually secret believers. The very nature of irregular war requires secrecy in almost all matters for the rebel. In any case secrecy and surprise have always been virtues in military matters—striking unexpectedly in unanticipated places. The rebel differs only in degree and in concealing the entire process of internal analysis from command decision through communication to post-operational consideration. When defeated, as are most revolutionary organizations and usually early on, few have shown great interest in the internal dynamics of their failure. When engaged in a campaign, few of the involved have time for analysis and even fewer observers—and almost never disinterested ones—can be concerned with the evolving tactical dynamics. After victory successful revolutionaries, like successful orthodox generals, tend to tidy up the past so as to fit theory and to buttress existing establishments. Although there is an enormous literature focused on unconventional war, the process involved in rebel target selection, the restraints, opportunities, and adjustments in evolving campaigns have eluded detailed analysis. Certainly, the rebel opponents have learned in the field a great many lessons, protected their own vulnerabilities and fashioned a counter-strategy to reduce the level of violence to tolerable levels while offering the alienated concessions labeled progress. And yet, even after long years of exposure, the conventional are often still surprised by an unexpected vulnerability, still confounded by rebel tactics in target selection.

There are various obstacles for the conventional when facing the unorthodox rebels, those motivated by a dream, gripped by an almost irrational optimism, and willing to take disproportionate risks with their lives and those of others. They are ever willing to persist in a war seemingly beyond winning, assured that history is theirs, that the people or the nation will sooner or later rise, that the weak will win. The rebels are not parallel if "secret" armies, much like their orthodox enemies, nor are they mirror images with all reversed, all permitted. They are not even cunning, secret guerrillas unhampered by the rules and regulations and cultural imperatives that limit the professional, the state soldier. They are *special*. Regardless of their ideology, rebels are all true believers, eager for power, all residents in a particular self-contained world. Each has a vision but few have adequate material resources other than their convictions. This unconventional world, inherently inefficient, limited by the necessity for secrecy, must rely on the unusual and unexpected even to persist, much less to escalate the campaign. To those in the underground the conventional have all the assets from that seat in the United Nations to a real medical service—all the things the rebel want. The wondrous guerrilla freedom appears very different to a rebel on the run, ill-armed, vulnerable, exhausted, hunted by skilled professionals. Such a rebel must first survive, persist and then, still without resources, find a means to act, by absolute necessity act secretly—to achieve with surprise the unexpected because the conventional is denied to him

Most revolutionary organizations share enormous limitations from—at the very core—an ideology, the formulation of a dream, in some matter flawed. Often that dream is denied by the proclaimed constituency unwilling to sacrifice for race or class or nation. There are as well tactical limits: the problems of command and control which must be either too rigid or too loose, the isolation of the underground, and the dearth of military resources. They always face the power of legitimacy and the professional skills of the more powerful enemy. In selecting targets all of these factors obviously limit options: for example (1) revolutionaries are severely limited by secrecy, not emboldened; (2) rebel communication is enormously difficult, often halting, always too cursory, without debate or even redundancy; (3) rebel command can rarely be effective or timely at a distance. Opportunities are lost because they cannot be reported, lost because they cannot be discussed, lost because they violate old orders, lost because of the very nature of the underground. And while each underground is the same, each is different, imposing special moral and political precedents and teaching various special historical lessons. Each rebel operates within a narrow but necessary underground of the mind, an underground structured by a special revolutionary dynamic, focused as much on persistence as on escalation. Each lives in an underground restricted by culture and historical experience both articulated and inherent. Thus every underground movement, regardless of ideology, size, campaign arena, opponent, prospects, or the moment in history, shares a certain dynamic, often largely recognized but often simply accepted as reality.

Each movement is also the end product of a long tradition. Even the most recent rebel has particular ancestors imposing certain values, demanding standards and offering witness and example. Each organization draws on a collective experience, sometimes long and rich, sometimes largely invented. All believe in their immediate history—and for the rebel history teaches certain, grand lessons, rules that have relevance in even the smallest matters of conduct. Generally, the past emboldens the rebel in great matters—the right of revolution—but tends to impose limits on lesser, tactical matters. A rebel has so few real assets that great care must be taken not to waste resources. The result, paradoxically, is that most revolutionary organizations are inherently conservative, suspicious of "stunts," of internally proposed novelties, of new directions. And, of course, the nature of covert organizations makes shifts difficult to accept and impose.

The great shadow over most organizations is the limitations on operations, on prospects, on options that is imposed by the lack of resources. What almost all revolutionary organizations want from their friends is first, always, always, arms—they never have enough and will even take tanks if offered (as did al-Fatah in Lebanon), or more rifles than they have active volunteers (as have the IRA); and, second—money; and last in every list—advice. To compensate for this inherent scarcity (later as the few successful movements grow larger, they also grow more conventional and may like Mao's end up as a regular army and an alternative government) the rebel is driven to tactics that will have an exaggerated and spectacular impact. Such acts are intended to be perceived by the "appropriate" audience as important even if the quantifiable result remains small. Some revolutionary organizations, like the People's Will, the Stern Group, Black September, had in fact terror strategies focused largely on symbolic operations, essentially strategies of perception. And thus faced with the restrictions of tradition, experience, conservatism, the limited resources, and always, the inherent inefficiency of underground organizations, the rebel's prospects must in part, often in large part, depend on revealed vulnerabilities, on the opponent's lapse or blunder. And at the end will come the improbable triumph of the will over entrenched and intractable power. At the end the center does not hold, pomp and power evaporate, history moves and the dream is vindicated. And the ultimate target—power—taken.

The Irish Republican Army

The recent Irish Republican experience reveals all of the anticipated dynamics of the underground; in fact, the Irish experience, longer than all and as intense as most, is in many ways a revolutionary archetype. The major rebel organization—the Provisional IRA—can trace its structural roots not just to the beginnings of the present Troubles in 1969 but also back through the old IRA of the Black-and-Tan years, 1918-1921 and after, to the Irish Volunteers of 1916 and on through the IRB to the Fenians. Ideologically the IRA is a descendant of Wolfe Tone's United Irishmen and of the ideas and ideals of the French revolution with only passing accretions of the class radicalism of the nineteenth century. Its practice has much of the atmosphere and attitudes of the island arena as well. At some point in the last two centuries, few strategies have not been deployed by Irish Republicans, few tactics not tried or tolerated. The IRA thus has an enormous memory of "history" as fashioned for present purpose. What has evolved on the island and in the American diaspora is not simply a movement or a secret army with a train of supporters but an Irish Republican world, fully Irish and so sharing all the nation's culture but also a world special, covert, accessible only to believers. It is a world dedicated to a dream, an ideal, and thus at least in part legitimate in many Irish eyes. It is a world not to be seen as an alternative government, not a party for a better Ireland, not even a movement of those of no property, but rather the receptacle of those who would still wage war for the ideal Republic currently discarded by the practical and everyday. They, the IRA, are not simply defenders of vulnerable Northern nationalists nor disgruntled working class radicals nor the residue of old crusades, but believers. They are, thus, abhorred by the content and conservative, often by most of the Irish, by all those who must deal in complexities, in daily life, in the practical. Everyone, not necessarily to advantage, has been touched by that Republican dream, often denied, generally discarded. Yet, somehow, generation after generation, the movement has been renewed by the faithful who have put the dream before reality, before practicality, moderation and propriety, before all else—and often they had little else.

Ideology

The dream, contradictory, denied by the many, impractical, supplies the energy to drive the Republican movement thus dedicated to a United Ireland, free and Gaelic. Such a Republic becomes real only on occasion for a few moments during a symbolic volley over the grave of a volunteer or along the country road outside Sallins in County Kildare when each June in celebration of Tone, buried at Bodenstown churchyard, the surrogates for the secret army emerge briefly. They are an outward and visible sign of the underground now twenty years on into their long war, two centuries after the long march began. Despite two centuries of futility, lost causes and only partial victories, there are still volunteers to march each year. Despite campaigns almost beyond number, murder from a ditch, arson, theft, extortion, inexcusable blunders, institutionalized incompetence, betrayal and schism, there are still those eager to serve the Republican dream. They now recognize most of the risks if not the prospect of a broken heart, often received in lieu of pension or medal. They, as volunteers in a brutal and mean crusade, are burdened by history, enhanced by past example, dedicated and determined in spite of all, because of all, all the tradition and experience and all the practice and all the old ideals. They carry with them into the IRA a past often misread, misused, misunderstood but never forgotten. And there in the underground, they at least know what is wrong with Ireland, what must be done, and what is to be won. In these sureties they are alone among all those involved in the Troubles. From their certainty the gift of the dream arises giving the power to persist.

First, the never failing source of all Irish political evils has always been the English connection. This artificial, imperialist link, maintained by power and guile, must be destroyed to free the nation. And, *second*, the only and appropriate means to do this is through physical force—the armed struggle—not through compromise nor conventional politics, not through petition nor civil protest nor occasional British concession. Victory with an Armalite assault rifle in one hand and a ballot-box in the other may be possible, has certainly been an amenable slogan to many Republicans not on active service, but the ballot-box alone is futile and any attempt to grasp such a ballot-box with the hand holding the rifle is a formula for disaster. The core assumption is that physical force exerted in the name of a Republic all but established in the hearts of the Irish is the key to the future. And if insufficient force is available, it is well to remember the words of Terence MacSwiney, who died on hunger strike in Brixton Prison, that "It is not those who can inflict the most, but those that can suffer the most who will conquer..." *Third*, when the Republic is established the common name of Irishmen will be substituted in place of the denomination of Protestant, Catholic, and Dissenter in a united, free island, freed from the curse of the English connection that divides and rules, freed by the persistent use of physical force. Those who would take less, the twenty-six counties of the present Republic or proposed British concessions in the North, those who seek a recess from violence or negotiation, those who foresee slaughter if there is forced unity, those who offer obstacles or cite British power or Loyalist intransigence or Irish timidity have no place among the true believers, each faithful to the dream. All revolutions look failures until the end. All face unsurmountable obstacles. All depend on the power of the dream over the enumerated assets of the state. So too the Irish Republicans.

The Organization

To transform this dream into a structure capable of affecting the course of history, the rebels have fashioned the movement, not an army, not a government-in-exile, not a party nor a subversive conspiracy but a covert world. The center is the IRA altered little in theoretical shape since the Black-and-Tan days. When the united Republican movement in the sixties began to move away from physical force, one of the first visible changes was the structure of the IRA—the size of the core was increased so that the advocates of a political direction could more easily control the future. When the movement split, formally, in 1969, first among individuals, then with a vote in the Sinn Féin Ard Fheis, and finally, formally, with the withdrawal of the traditionalists from the Army Convention to form the real IRA at a Provisional Army Convention in December—hence Provos—the form remained. The Official IRA ever so gradually discarded the gun, the old form, the strictures of Republicanism and became transmuted into the Workers Party. A journey that saw still another split and the formation of the Irish National Liberation Army (INLA) with the political Irish Republican Socialist Party (IRSP) that retained much of the form of the past, if in recent times only in military titles for pathological gunmen. Of course, in every case, as is true with almost all organizations, the theoretical forms did not necessarily indicate the actuality of power, responsibility, and control. Still, the inherited form was felt valuable, and this remains so with the IRA.

The IRA is structured as a democratic, if secret, army, power in theory flowing from the volunteers into the center. The army should at least every other year elect delegates to the Army Convention but because of the current armed struggle this has been possible only three times: in the beginning in 1969 and 1970 to establish the alternative to the "Officials" and a third time in October 1986. This was to impose the arranged consensus that ended abstentionism and produced another schism with Republican Sinn Féin, who hold as principle the view that Westminster and Leinster House, like Stormont, has no legitimacy, could provide no forum for true Republicans. These Army Conventions, like most Army Conventions, including the one that the Provos left in 1969, had been called by a leadership that controlled the system and hence the majority. In the case of the current IRA, the Executive elected in September 1970 had continued, filling positions by co-option, until October 1986, when a new one was elected.

In general the twelve-man Executive, which usually meets twice a year, is an advisory body that selects the army Council, the key and core of the IRA, repository of legitimacy and power, whose membership has been maintained by co-option. This Council in secret chooses a Chief of Staff who then selects his own staff—a number two Adjutant General, a Quartermaster General, often a Director of Operations, officers for finance, publicity, intelligence—whatever may be needed. At times the C/S has been the dominant figure in the army, at others not. The key operational figure for a decade has usually been the O/C Northern Command, a structure set up to bring local control to the Northern arena. Influential or talented local O/Cs are usually in time co-opted onto the Army Council. The dominance of the C/S has declined, as has the influence and importance of those in the South.

Mostly the IRA has been dominated at the top by very few commanders, one to three, who are associated on the Army Council or Executive with colleagues they have known for years, often a lifetime. Real power, based on consensus, tacit agreement, like minds, remains at the center within the Army Council, the nexus of the system and still for some the legitimate government of Ireland.

Outside the vague edges of the secret army, there are other Republicans and Republican organizations: Sinn Féin, legal if harassed, North and South, the political arm whose members from time to time have pretensions of power that can never be discounted, the newspaper *An Phoblacht*, the dependants' fund, the groups in the American diaspora, the various Irish committees, spokesmen, ad hoc groups, and support structures, often in the diaspora, always meeting in bleak halls to protest, to encourage, to give witness. Many often act with considerable independence—even competing at times for resources. All are, however, committed to the armed struggle and in this are supported by a collection of invisible Republicans, those without records, often those with other public views, those who will look the other way or supply a house, those who give secretly or whose only visible service is to pass along the word or watch the end of the lane. All in the end are answerable to the Army Council. And the Army Council, meeting once or twice a month for a few hours, often in safe houses along the border or some place in the Republic, operates on consensus, rarely finding fault with the commanders in the field, and is rarely called upon to fine tune operations or to change strategic directions. Rarely, in fact, does the Army Council vote: for, whatever else, Irish Republicans tend to know their own mind.

Consensus, then, at the top, is the IRA rule on substantive matters, even among very different men with vastly different personalties. Most are and have been men of no property, limited men, narrow in politics, restricted in experience, seldom with access to technical or intellectual talent. The IRA is working class with a sprinkling of the more traditional radical class—the lower middle class of clerks, school teachers, the ambitious and disgruntled. After a generation of the current armed struggle, some volunteers have spent their lives within the movement. At times the IRA has been dominated by a single figure like Seán MacStiofáin from 1969 to 1972, while at others there has been little control from the center—Joe Cahill spent most of his brief tenure as C/S in 1972-1973 out of the country. In the twenty years of the current campaign, those involved in the leadership for any length of time, almost inevitably on the Army Council, have numbered not much more than a score—at most— giving the organization a remarkable continuity. Most have been well known even outside the movement—MacStiofáin, Ruairí Ó Brádaigh, Daithí Ó Conaill, Billy McKee, J. B. O'Hagen, Seamus Twomey, Brian Keenan, Gerry Adams, Martin McGuinness, Ivor Bell and a few others plus the less well known, less visible, some old faithfuls, some retired. Almost all have spent a lifetime within the movement so that their responses, attitudes, assumptions, and predilections have been shaped by their Republican faith: there are few apostates and those mostly are to be found in the Workers Party.

Within the IRA Army Council there have been three generations. First were IRA people, especially from Belfast, active in the forties as young volunteers. Then there were those like Ó Brádaigh, Ó Conaill, Bell or Kevin Mallon of the campaign years of 1954-1962. In those years they had as colleagues Seamus Costello, who appeared as C/S of the INLA and Seán Garland who remained in the Officials. Finally there are the volunteers of 1969-1972 who came of age in the mid-seventies. All the same, all different, they were a mix whose attitudes had been shaped by differing conditions, levels of tolerations, degrees of humiliation and anger. At the center of the Provisional IRA, there were urban and rural Republicans, radicals and conservatives in politics and aspirations, young and old—not all '50s men were ancient or '69 volunteers young. There were in the North women as well who wanted to be real, active service volunteers—and were, at times, in significant roles.

Even the most innocent volunteer, eager for a gun, eager to defend, without a grasp of history or an interest in politics, became sooner rather than later a Republican, a true believer, a member of the convert world united on the dream, agreed on the basics. Some lost faith. Some did not stay the route. Some were corrupted or corrupt. Thousands became volunteers and not all were paragons or idealists; but many, most, were touched by the dream. After 1969 most of the volunteers were young, working-class, increasingly from the North, various in character and tastes, very Irish, usually devout and—of course—almost never Protestant, deeply nationalist. In a group seemingly diverse, sullen or gay, city wise or country stupid, reflective or abubble, tall and short, poorly educated with a few readers, all were different but all caught in history, all living in the secret Republican world: and all because of their background on a small, homogeneous island, because of their shared assumptions and convictions, were much the same. And year after year no matter the blunders of the leadership, the skills of the security forces, no matter the risks and the pleas of fearful parents, the volunteers continued to appear. There were fewer in the South, where there was neither action nor role, few in the North where only so many active service people could be deployed but always ample for the movement's purpose. Some, like Adams, who came from a Belfast Republican family, and McGuinness, who knew so little of the movement that in October 1970 he first appeared at the Officials' door, moved in time into the leadership. Thousands ended in prison, some for life, hundreds were killed and maimed, most passed through active service—a young person's career—and out with convictions unchanged but no real role other than to give a vote, buy a newspaper, offer a bed and a kind word. And year after year, mostly with the same men in the same chairs, the Army Council oversaw the campaign while the operations officers directed the same volunteers until arrest or exhaustion or a fatal error opened a slot for the next in line.

Strategy

The great decision of the Army Council in January 1970 had been to use the turmoil and trouble to move into an armed struggle by three stages: (1) Nationalist Defender—organize and arm a "militia" secret army; (2) Retaliation made possible by gradually provoking the British security forces so that they would alienate the nationalists—almost, the Army Council felt, a given for any British army quartered on the Irish; (3) thus allowing the IRA as a secret urban-rural guerrilla army to engage the British whenever and wherever possible with the accumulated arms and the new and trained volunteers. Creating a constituency, building an army adequately equipped for the task, provoking a skilled opponent into classical errors and exploiting Northern reality to undertake a serious and costly armed struggle was a remarkable achievement. An achievement planned by a score of men with limited talents, no money, few prospects, irregularly meeting in shoddy rooms, begining in 1970—an incredible achievement when the dream of an armed campaign turned into a real war in 1971, waged by those same men. When the British sent heavily armed troops into the IRA no-go zones in Belfast and Derry in July 1972, there were ninety-five deaths. In the previous four months there had been 5,500 shooting incidents. Hundreds of bombs, many hidden in cars, had turned the centers of most Northern Irish towns into rubble. The roads were not safe from ambush nor the police able to enter nationalist areas. In March London had closed down the provincial government at Stormont, symbol North and South of Orange sectarian rule. In July 1972, the IRA representatives had met with the British in London—bombed their way to bargaining. When, on July 9, the truce collapsed, the shooting war began again. Anyone could stand on the street in

Belfast any day and hear the crack of IRA rifles and the thump of car bombs: physical force with a vengeance directed by an Army Council hidden away beyond British reach and largely beyond analysis.

Tactics

The Provos in 1972 had their campaign, one that would continue through various phases for a generation but never at the same high level of intensity: 103 members of the British Army killed, 24 from the Ulster Defence Regiment and 14 from the Royal Ulster Constabulary and 3 from the police reserve—a real war in the middle of the United Kingdom. And over the following generation the command structure of the IRA remained largely the same, the key direction by two or three men, often in place over a long period of time. Although in time and slowly, the level of operational efficiency increased, as did the variety and location of IRA targets, mostly the factors encouraging or limiting certain choices remained remarkably stable. Well before 1972 a consensus existed on priorities and limitations, a consensus rarely discussed and at times unrecognized by the involved. Such general, unspoken agreement meant that the traditional and insoluble problem of all underground organizations—control at the operational point by the center—was eased even if the results were often less than desirable. Generally, the units in the field knew target possibilities and priorities without need for central monitoring. An increase in intensity might be required by the C/S or a truce imposed by the Army Council but rarely was there need to shift or to deny target priorities—although local actions often focused on certain vulnerabilities or symbols or special categories without central instruction. These "new" priorities were most often dictated by opportunity, by very local considerations, by the need to explain what had been undertaken without much, if any, tactical or strategic planning. Sometimes new targets would be selected at the center; but often these, too, would be obvious and almost always within the usual parameters of action regularly related to campaign priorities. Thus, for twenty years the Provos had much the same structure, ran a campaign limited and inspired by much the same factors. IRA strategy could be explained, if at all, as a revolutionary constant from the first Army Council to the present. To the IRA their strategy was obvious, their tactics congenial, their targets easily explicable.

Republican Alternatives

Over the generation of Troubles almost the reverse was true with the Official IRA, the radical Republicans cored in Dublin and the old 1968 GHQ, who transformed a covert, illicit armed movement into a conventional parliamentary party, mostly in the Irish Republic with branches in the North. The old Republican ideology was discarded for a relatively rigid Marxist-Leninist posture, the old IRA structure was discarded for an overt party controlled by democratic centralism and the skills of the old people, rather than by the new radical recruits. The old gunmen were retired, or, as a hidden

IRA, secretly put to work protecting illicit fund raising in Belfast and acquiring party funds through armed robberies, often in the Republic. Thus Official Sinn Féin became Sinn Féin—The Workers Party, and at last the Workers Party with a member in the European Parliament, a delegation in the Dáil in Dublin and a tiny presence in the North—a party opposed to terror, to the Provos, to recollecting their own militant nationalist past. With the changes in Eastern Europe in 1989, the party even promised Irish *glasnost* and Celtic *perestroika* The shift to such politics over the years was reflected in both the actual structure of their IRA and in the nature of its "military" operations. In 1968 the Dublin GHQ had increased the size of the "Army Council" as a means of diluting formal power so that GHQ could not be trapped into unwanted militancy. Thus the old forms could be eased away through democratic reform. In effect the old IRA forms were kept for some time, the Army Convention was still meeting in the eighties: nevertheless the military wing of the movement was run down, run down rapidly after 1972. In May 1972, without GHQ authorization, the Officials in Derry killed a young man, Ranger William Best, home on leave from the British Army, even, according to some, eager to desert. The local outcry at the brutality was intense and GHQ in Dublin took the opportunity to declare a truce on May 29. While many of the Northern volunteers continued to carry out independent operations, often crediting the Provos, and many members of the organization continued to favor some sort of armed action, from that time on the Officials moved out of the army business. The truce continued, became policy, and in time many Officials, as Workers, chose to forget past involvement in the armed struggle. The small Official IRA became a secret army, secret not only from the authorities but also from the new radicals of the Workers Party. IRA control had always rested in Dublin GHQ, more so than in the Provisionals where the Army Council and/or Northern Command had a continuing role in a much larger organization. From 1970 this GHQ consisted of only three or four men just as by the eighties the Official IRA, long denied, consisted only of small units in Belfast and Newry in the North and a couple of dozen individuals, in time not all IRA volunteers, mostly involved in expropriation out of Dublin. In theory no "military" action was taken without Dublin-GHQ authorization.

The double levels of secrecy, the strains imposed by schisms and splits (most Official operations after 1972 were directed at fellow Irish Republicans), and differences in temperament and priorities of those at the center of the circle in Dublin meant, however, that without the old forms and Republican priorities, control could be lax and divided.

Over the generation of the Troubles two other small but often very violent groups emerged from the Republicans—or their aura. The first was Saor Éire, ideologically, if anything, "Trotskyite," a flag of convenience for radicals opposed to any orthodox radicalism. The movement was a mix of narrow ideologists, opportunists, and the freelance gunmen that chaos permits. The movement was involved in bank robberies with the returns not always ending in party funds. It proved so ephemeral that neither the Officials nor the

Provos ever sought to close it down. Far more significant was the breakaway from the Officials led by the charismatic Republican Seamus Costello, unwilling to watch the IRA closed down and unsympathetic to those at the core of the Officials. He was eager for radical action instead of a withdrawal into everyday politics. On December 8, 1974, at the Spa Hotel in Lucan, he formed with like-minded radical nationalists the IRSP and, simultaneously and secretly upstairs, the INLA.

The inevitable disputes over heresy and arms dumps produced open war in Belfast and unresolved friction between the Officials and INLA. In the meantime Costello dominated the INLA armed struggle, supported by a small political cast, mostly in the South, and a variety of Belfast gunmen, mostly old Officials but also some new recruits alienated by the Provos and eager for action. The INLA carried out a series of spectaculars—the most dramatic being a car bomb that killed Margaret Thatcher's friend and adviser on Ireland, Airey Neave, in 1979 as he drove out of the parliamentary carpark at Westminster. The INLA was dominated by Costello even until the Official feud ended. He was murdered in Dublin on October 5, 1977. The IRSP-INLA was soon decimated. The Loyalists in the North killed as many of the political figures as they could reach, and the active service people, without Costello's discipline, in time proved largely ineffectual except during internal feuds. There were arrests in the South and policy divisions North and South. Then the remaining gunmen, unsavory, deadly, engaged in a murderous feud, killed off most of the activists by the spring of 1988. Essentially Costello, charismatic, ruthless, determined, had held the INLA together—once he was gone most of the radicals wanted no part of an armed campaign and most of the gunmen nothing but a chance to kill. Although the IRSP-INLA was more important, more long-lived than Saor Éire, more serious, it really did not effectively survive Costello long. The forms adopted from orthodox republicans and the ill-digested radical ideals were not sufficient to allow institutional control nor to produce a legitimate leadership succession.

Essentially since the spring of 1972, the crucial player in the armed struggle has been the Provisional IRA—now *the* IRA. The other Irish Republicans when engaged in the armed struggle tended to reflect Provo priorities if not parallel means of command and control. Saor Éire operated not unlike a robber band, akin to the later Euro-terrorists but with fewer ideological strings. The INLA was run like a mini-Provisional IRA by a dominating Chief of Staff who needed little consensus, since his volunteers sought mostly any sort of action and his radicals as little as possible. The Official IRA kept traces of the form but little of the function of the old days and was dominated by a core group within the old GHQ staff in Dublin. The Provos were, then, the crucial component in the campaign against the British for over twenty years, directing over ten thousand operations on the island, in England, on the continent, maintaining contacts within the diaspora, especially the United States, and in the Middle East. The Provisional IRA evolved into one of the world's premier revolutionary organizations despite inherent faults and failures, despite institutionalized incapacities, despite limited talent and a narrow vision. And all during this period the scope, nature, and importance of the IRA's targets remained relatively stable: the priorities of 1969 or 1972 were still valid twenty years later. The IRA, no matter the radical ideas and ideals of its militants, remains essentially a conservative underground, slow to shift military priorities, slow to cope with technological escalation, unsophisticated, persistent, embedded in history and practice, still targeted on the congenial—a constant in a radically shifting world.

The Dynamic of IRA Strategy and Tactics

A revolutionary organization must organize and deploy the available assets, from enthusiasm to smuggled pistols, in a coherent strategy that assures persistence and promises escalation. Almost from the first the rebel accepts material inferiority, a limitation alleviated by the possession of a just cause and on a reading of history that assures in time the will of the denied will overcome the assets of the center. Many organizations must invest—or feel the need to invest—much time in devising an ideologically correct strategy or a morally just course of action: this may descend to details, the appropriate make of automobile to steal for a bomb, or rise to an exegesis on tyrannicide. Little time is devoted to the practical concerns of most analysts seeking analogies with counter-insurgency concerns, with military parallels, with a conventional agenda. The rebel spends the very little time remaining that is not invested in persistence under pressure in relating the dream to the demands of reality. The IRA spends even less in consideration of strategic options or tactical initiatives. The long history, the accepted wisdom of the immediate past, the unspoken consensus means that most decisions have been made. The Army Council or the individual volunteers may contemplate the speed the strategic process takes, the year of victory or a twenty-year war, in power by Christmas or by the next century, but rarely the appropriate means to achieve the organizational goals. The formal strategic decisions came only at the very beginning in the plan to move from organization for defense to open war; after the armed struggle emerged in 1971, all traditional means of escalation were welcome and almost no novelties arose from the ranks. By 1971, in any case, the movement was intimate with a long tactical past that taught whatever lessons the Army Council chose to learn.

The tactical decisions of the IRA, usually taken on a local level, often authorized at GHQ or the Army Council, sometimes after the fact, tend to focus on the possible and immediate means of escalating. Operations can engage more and different local targets, move beyond the existing arena, require more elegant or at least different arms, but are almost always logical, within past tradition, easy to accept and often relatively easy to undertake at first. Most particularly there has been an effort to find the vulnerable—persistence has installed caution as well as skill in the active service volunteers, sometimes to technical disadvantage when risks are required for appropriate effect. With time the IRA volunteer has become more adept, a growth largely cancelled by the evolving skills of the British opponent, but remains hampered by a lack of technological skill, a cultural heritage unsympathetic to precision, and an innocence once off home ground. In part there is compensation from surprise, from the enormous perceived damage that a few may do to complex systems, and from the ingenuity of the individuals involved. By intention, by accident, by design or by luck, the novel tactics, mostly adjustments from the past, have an immediate impact, grow stale, are added to the lexicon of violence and have a diminishing return, thus requiring more novelty.

This process can be seen at work in the gradual evolution of IRA bombs from the early 1970 devices reminiscent of the anarchists of the previous century to the far more sophisticated current constructions that can endanger a target for months or defy detection by all but the most sophisticated trackers. The new bombs are elegant, dangerous, and allow persistence rather than promise escalation—tactically the IRA has barely managed to stand still. Much the same is the case with other initiatives and adjustments: letter bombs, car bombs, trap-bombs, proxy bombs, bombs from fertilizer or courtesy of Libyan Semtex but never a device or a target that transforms the struggle. Tactics are adjustments to pressure, to opportunity, to the edges of the arena. Tactics are so intimately woven into the struggle that novelty is rare. And all the novel tactics, like the old ones, are fashioned so that the armed struggle may *first* persist, persist until the will wins over the entrenched assets of the Crown, and *second* escalate, escalate until the Crown will no longer pay the cost. And almost no one in operations or in authority within the IRA spends much time discussing matters beyond techniques, the potential level of intensity, and perceived vulnerabilities—and such matters almost never engender dispute, much less a vote in the Army Council. Megastrategy is for academics or military schools.

IRA Targets

People
Like most sensible armies, legitimate or covert, the IRA has as a prime target the enemy in general—them, the other army and its supporters, *people*. And since the IRA is in name at least an "army" then the primary target is the other army, them, the British Army, uniformed, booted, polished and professional. One of the great failures of the 1956-1962 IRA campaign was that the few active service volunteers could never come to grips with the other army but only with their surrogates the police, the Royal Ulster Constabulary. In all those years six RUC men were killed but no soldier. In the current campaign the whole strategy in the years 1969-1971 was to lure the British Army into a real war with the IRA, the nationalist defenders. So first and foremost and always, the military forces of Britain remain the prime target. At home, at play, out of uniform, in retirement, shopping or commuting, any member of the British army remains at risk; for the IRA seeks the man or woman, not the uniform. And in this in part ideological priority is obvious. One of the reasons that the astute in London have sought to "criminalize" the IRA campaign by shifting the major security burden onto the police is to move away from a war. There then would be no IRA war, just a police matter, an Irish matter, not a war at all. And so by reducing the British army presence whenever possible, London lets the Irish manage the police, and the police manage the police reserve. One set of Irish is killing the other: tribal murder not war.

The Irish Troubles are, of course, not war or not conventional war so that the IRA target list is somewhat irregular. While an IRA volunteer would prefer an operation against a uniformed patrol, any members of the security service—army, navy, police, coast guard, tea-boy—in uniform or out, will serve. An RUC reserve constable sitting on a tractor plowing his field is not simply an Armagh farmer nor a Presbyterian nor a father at home watched by his children but also and mainly a member of the British security forces. So he is shot off the tractor, not as farmer or Protestant or father but as a vulnerable soldier. In fact within the nationalist community, such IRA priorities cause some unease—the further from a real military action, a shoot-out with an army patrol, and the closer to tribal murder, a part-time RUC reservist shot on his doorstep, the greater the unease. Within the IRA ranks there may be those who are not as nonsectarian as ideology requires or even as eager to open up on the paratroopers; but within the IRA command structure there is no doubt and no difference admitted—in uniform or out, female or male, at work or at play, the security forces, these people, are a proper and prime target. And such targets have been traced and attacked in London streets, at country houses, in European cities, in bus lines and supermarkets, asleep or awake. In real war the B-52s don't wait until the target rises, puts on a uniform, and thus becomes a legitimate target. Why should the IRA in Tyrone or Knightsbridge? The horse guard riding by Hyde Park, a military band school in Kent or the Armagh constable are thus prime targets—the more unsuspecting the better for the volunteer.

If the cutting edge of the enemy is seen as the security forces, it is clear that their political masters, their bureaucratic colleagues, some members of parliament (like the late Ian Gow) and all security support systems, are no less crucial. In general, although not always in particular, government employees in some way directly involved in supporting the security forces, in particular military departments and those suspected of intelligence activities, no matter how innocuous, are to the IRA commanders obvious targets. Post officials, custom officials, police caterers, clerks in the Northern Irish Office, may be targeted either singly—for some reason attracting the interest of an IRA unit—or as a category—for specific and often publicly announced reasons. During the confrontation within the prisons in 1980-1982, prison warders and officials were especial targets: some as individuals noted for particular acts but all as part of the judicial system that transported on a conveyor belt IRA suspects into prison on uncertain evidence. In an elaboration of a campaign directed against the construction of security barracks for the RUC, various contractors and their workers were warned that they would be targets. This list was expanded to include anyone involved in the process of construction or fitting the stations, a campaign so effective that at times army engineers had to be used and there was a pronounced unease even for those workers refilling coke machines. What can occur is a rippling effect from the soldier through the service economy on out to an irrational distance: the sergeant, his barber, and the razor salesman. There are enemies—targets—the IRA does not want: Irish, working class, neighbours. Ideologically this is undesirable, increasingly irrational; but such a process opens softer and softer targets and may still be "rationalized" if an active service unit feels the need. The IRA constituency may accept the reasoning—and the enemy as always will cry cowardice, madness, more criminal murders.

The IRA has faced a serious ideological problem with the emergence of Protestant paramilitary organizations—illegal, indiscriminate, militantly loyalist even when sought and arrested by their own British army. The Protestant bands, the Red Hand Commandos or the Ulster Freedom Fighters, are often cover names for legal organizations and often have elaborate titles for what are ill-organized gangs of militant vigilantes. At times their members are driven by psychological pressures or irrational personal hatreds rather than motivated by political or military concerns. Since 1972 the major violent activity of the loyalist paramilitaries has been to strike at the subversive traitors, *them*, the nationalists, Irish, Catholic, Republicans, all disloyal so all the equivalent of the IRA. A great many vulnerable Catholic males without politics or connections with the Republican movement have been killed or wounded and some brutally tortured first. More discrete loyalists have sought as targets the political figures on the other side of the divide— much of the small political leadership of the IRSP was shot by loyalist paramilitaries, the Vice-President of Sinn Féin, Máire Drumm, was murdered in her hospital room, and the President of Sinn Féin, Gerry Adams, was shot but escaped death in an attack on his car in central Belfast.

The problem ideologically for the IRA is that all of these Irishmen should be not enemies but class and national allies—and after two centuries there are still those within the movement who await the conversion of the loyalist working class. As a non-sectarian organization, albeit one nearly entirely Catholic and identified with Irish Catholic nationalism, the IRA does not want "Protestant" enemies and so, particularly at first, defined the loyalists as agents of British imperialism. Since the role of nationalist (i.e. Catholic) defender remains a basic part of the IRA appeal, the loyalist gunmen must at times be a target. A few Loyalists are so well known or prominent that, even if reluctantly, operations against the guilty can be undertaken. Many of the sectarian killers are unknown, however, and local pressure has from time to time "forced" IRA units to undertake tit-for-tat killings, some swift and brutal and even effective, and some leading to a series of mutual murders.

At times the Army Council or GHQ or Northern Command simply ignored the retaliation, even denied any IRA involvement—after all no one, no IRA unit, asked them for permission. No one in Republican authority has ever been easy about Protestants as targets, preferring to make the loyalist paramilitaries into British army auxiliaries or victims of spontaneous local nationalist vengeance. And most specifically no one in IRA authority wants volunteers killing Protestants with enthusiasm in the name of past grievance and present distaste—which is, alack for ideology, sometimes the case. Protestants as Protestants are the people-target of last choice—should not be targets at all.

The most crucial people-target, more so than major-generals or members of the Westminster cabinet, for the IRA, for any revolutionary organization are the informers. For the military, cowardice is the great professional sin, for scholars plagiarism, but for revolutionaries it is informing, betraying the power of the dream. An informer casts doubt on the faith and the faithful—a revolutionary must trust his own, his ideals, their power to inspire. Consequently, there is always a miasma of suspicion even at the heart of the movement, fear of the unknown devil, who would, beyond the measurable damage of arrests, ambushes set, aborted operations, lost dumps, also contaminate the faith. Thus IRA informers are a prime target, some—misguided, young, vulnerable, well-connected in the parish— permitted to flee the country. Those only slightly guilty may be only partially punished, beaten, tarred-and-feathered, shot in the leg. The real informers, however, end at the back of the lane or on the side of the road, sprawled in a black plastic bag, witness and warning and target. Betrayal from without, police spies, touts, criminals selling information to the police, informers with conscience, schismatic political opponents, felon setters out of malice, are always targets but with no set rules for punishment—only the prospect of death or maiming. The IRA have no prisons, no system that permits much leniency, and must like all rebels act directly, violently. External informers—unless a massive escalation in betrayal indicates an enormous decay in local support—are not as crucial a target as the traitor from within, the one rotten apple that may spoil the barrel. Always the informer, the obverse of the devout, must be sought, targeted, eradicated, dumped as witness.

A final category of targets often seems as vital to remove as the informer and, at first at least, as ideologically difficult as the loyalist paramilitaries: the heretics. Withdrawing into private life is an IRA convention; retirement because of exhaustion, because of policy disagreements, because of any reasonable compulsion, is tolerated, even encouraged, but not the organization of internal or external opposition. Schism in covert, revolutionary organizations is often very bitter. The possession of the dream is at stake—and most dreams are indivisible. And most such organizations do split. One of the inherent penalties of the underground is schism. Attempts to seize the movement from within rarely lead to violence if aborted, and regularly lead to violence if an alternative movement is established. Often the splinter has the same or a similar constituency, a deadly challenge, and often a different military strategy, an insufferable affront. Thus the Provisional and Official IRA engaged in a shooting feud as did the Officials and Costello's INLA—as do the various, shifting and hazy loyalist paramilitary movements. Only if the heretic retires has there been toleration. Thus the 1985 split in Sinn Féin between those still in favor of refusing to take parliamentary seats in London or Dublin and those who would do so for tactical purpose. The abstentionists withdrew and formed Republican Sinn Féin, their own party. A "party" is not a movement and the schismatics did not try and organize an army—and were warned not to make such a move. Thus they could be tolerated as a lost and misguided tribe. If the split grows to involve the IRA, the armed struggle, then violence is likely just as in the past. The Officials could not tolerate the INLA people seceding and taking their guns nor, previously, the Officials and Provos the provocative presence of an alternative army.

Essentially, inter-Republican feuding has absorbed an enormous amount of time and left many participants incredibly bitter, but in contrast to schisms elsewhere it has cost relatively few lives. Quite often more rebel volunteers, more of the faithful, are killed by their own than by security forces—for the future belongs to those who possess the dream, the high ground of revolution, not to mention the arms dumps and the awe of the people. At times, then, in Ireland, the first target of Irish Republicans has been Irish Republicans and given appropriate conditions could yet be so again.

Beyond the categories of targets, building contractors, informers or heretics, there are specific individual targets, people attacked because they are someone very special, symbolize a general foe. An individual may, of course, be dangerous, possess special knowledge, have special talents, be difficult to replace as a functionary, and thus be precisely targeted. Some positions—certain police and army slots, certain military commanders, certain heretics (the "other" chief of staff)—assure targeting. Mostly, as well, these particular jobs have a high visibility and the individual through his professional enthusiasm and special skills may attract attention not simply for his role but also for his public portrayal: almost all generals commanding Northern Ireland have been targets but some are more congenial IRA targets than others because of reputation, public posture, or even a particular television appearance or policy statement.

As the recognition of the individual increases, not just a general but General Frank Kitson, founder of modern British anti-insurgency theory, so does the symbolic value of such a target. Any British ambassador may do, but in 1976 the new man in Dublin, who had a history of intelligence connections, who was the first really serious man appointed to Ireland, and who appeared as a bonus to be a stock British imperial character, cunning, devious, eccentric, and elegant, was obviously a more congenial target, would return symbolic as well as functional dividends. Thus Margaret Thatcher with her arrogant and grating assurance, with her complicity in the death of the hunger strikers, with her *nouveau*-talented conservatives, anti-Irish, neo-imperialist, was an ideal symbolic target where folksy, friendly, congenial James Callaghan would have been considerably less so. Hence a very specific effort was made to kill Margaret Thatcher, vengeance achieved, a cabinet killed, a nation threatened, a government gone—an ideal target. And much the same was the case with Lord Mountbatten, who in Irish Republican circles engendered no love as a grand old man of empire, steeped in honor and cousin to royalty. English lords, even old ones, have in any case a small Irish constituency. Living with limited security in a war zone, arrogant among the Paddies, imperial symbol, well-beloved by those whose attention to Irish matters tended to wander, he was for the IRA an ideal individual target. His assassination, producing such outraged indignation in the United Kingdom, indicated a target well taken. In fact some of the active service units in Britain, holed up with little to do, spend hours thumbing over reference works, working up lists of potential targets of all sorts and condition: military chaplains, advocates of harsh counter-measures, generals and politicians and five-star restaurants; check marks in categories, check marks against symbols, and some possible targets that are hard to explain—random, bored checks. In any case symbolic assassination—Mountbatten had almost no power and Thatcher all that is available to an individual—has always been a revolutionary means and is no less so for the IRA.

Places

Just like real armies, the IRA has often found targets in places, occupied or empty. These target sites tend to parallel the vulnerable people. Thus all military and security facilities are obvious targets, prime enemy resources, the more obvious when filled with people but better hit when empty than not at all. Mostly but not always, the operations against facilities are intended to inflict casualties. After all such operations are as great a risk if the target is empty as if it is full. At times, however, soft security targets can be hit: isolated microwave towers, partially built barracks, empty customs posts. And at times the operation can be such that few casualties can really be anticipated—leaving a car-bomb in an army parking lot. Since the authorities must respond at some cost and at great inconvenience—and at real risk—to each attack, there is an inclination by the

IRA to define security targets broadly, including communication facilities, catering warehouses, construction sites—secondary and soft targets, auxiliary facilities. And, as in the case with people, these target groups move on out—court houses, prison garages, bus depots, the Dublin-Belfast railway line. All in some way can be considered security targets. All, when hit, require a security response—and often repairs and readjustment by the army or police. All, thus, fit the IRA's target preferences. In particular this is true because the IRA commanders do the defining of what is an appropriate security target and what is not: a lumber yard that sells to a contractor who erects the scaffolding for repairs to a tax office becomes an "appropriate" target no matter what the newspapers or army spokesmen or Republican rivals may say. As the physical target becomes divorced from the security forces, from real war, even from war industry, then a secondary campaign is cited as relevant: the destruction of the artificial economy of the Six Counties.

The bombing began in 1970-1971, at first without the IRA taking responsibility, as much because it was possible, would engender chaos, would provoke the security forces, would employ the volunteers, would hasten the advent of a real campaign, as the result of any great strategic decision or elaborate rationale. Explosives, at first made in Jack McCabe's garage in Dublin and smuggled north, were available and so were simply used—all but automatically—to intensify British problems. The avowed target—the Northern economy—came later, and in time included almost any object that could be bombed away, stores, houses, hotels, bridges, boats, war monuments, the lot. And all sorts of devices were developed, from diabolic devices sputtering fire from a fuse as they were rushed into a tailor's shop, to complex detonators that could be operated automatically by electronic timers months after the bomb had been plastered into a wall or dug into a garden.

In time the centers of most Northern towns were marred by rubble. The remaining hotels were protected by barbed wire, electronic devices and troops. The center of Belfast was sealed off with a security-zone fence and special gates. Many roads were never safe. Many businesses never reopened. Many innocent people as well as members of the security forces were killed or maimed: warnings not given or given too late, premature explosions or crowds too close to the action. Thousands and thousands of bombs, constructed from chemicals, from stolen or imported explosives, timed by ever more sophisticated devices, were detonated by increasingly professional devices—and countermeasures aborted nearly as many operations as the IRA successfully directed. In fact, since almost everything in Northern Ireland could be a target, the relative normality of the towns and countryside after twenty years of bombing is remarkable. And bombing is no longer easy but simply possible, even if the massive blitzes of 1972 can not be repeated. Thus IRA bomb targets currently tend to have more specific rationalizations. As long as a bomb is to be used, best it be planted on some important or symbolic objective. And even if the targets are soft—hotels—best that a more complex or compelling rationale be devised such as the destruction of the artificial tourist industry or the destruction of recreation facilities used by the British Army.

In the case of bombing operations in England, there is no hope of maintaining a high-level, intensive campaign. In fact, by the 1980s, operations in England had become as difficult as, if not more difficult than, those on the continent. The Irish diaspora in England, never as in America a hotbed of Republican support, has been closely monitored for years. All immigrants, internal or external, are watched, especially those from certain Irish areas—Belfast or South Armagh—or with any subversive connections. The British police and public are vigilant, wary, and hardly produce a friendly ocean for IRA fish. And the skills and talents of the active service units have often been limited: innocent, unsophisticated, poorly trained Irish lads—and from time to time women—with no real knowledge of England, the English, or of any but their own. Thus English targets are usually soft, the volunteers often careless about civilian life, and the burst of activity usually ended by arrests. The targets, if possible, are soft security—troop buses, military canteens, minor barracks, a military band, and a bar frequented by off duty soldiers. Often the casualties turn out to be civilians who have replaced the off-duty soldiers, or catering staff, not paratroopers but bystanders.

The second, more general, campaign is to cause chaos within the center, usually central London with scattershot forays against targets as diverse as the Tower of London and Harrods. Elegant clubs and fashionable restaurants become imperialist centers and fast food stores on Oxford Street "appropriate" economic targets. Mostly the intention is to attract attention, bring the war home to the English, cause trouble. The targets, so many targets in a vast city under siege from six or eight IRA volunteers, are everywhere vulnerable and available. Yet swift and complex responses by the police often make supposedly vulnerable areas of London—the West End—much less vulnerable than the IRA volunteers could imagine. Finally, beyond soft security and general chaos categories, the IRA has added in certain symbolic targets, those with both function and emotive content, for example a bomb at former Prime Minister Edward Heath's London home.

Mostly there is a feeling within the IRA that any attack within England has a high symbolic content, carries a message and the war closer, attracts wavering attention. In the case of the first London car-bombs, in 1973, when the volunteers were arrested at the airport on their way back to Ireland, the explosions overshadowed the plebiscite on the border, a foregone loyalist victory, capturing the front pages and outraging popular opinion. The bombs ruined an exercise by the British government to reassure their own. Thus English targets, soft or hard, do not fall as easily into categories since the *place* is the major factor—a British soldier killed in London is more important than his security category because of the site of the operation. Obviously people count, too, and military targets and symbolic assassinations; but the place is important so much so that grave risks to the innocent are tolerated if not encouraged. This has resulted in feckless murder, classical terror, rather than in the death of civilians through incompetence that has marred the Six-County IRA record. War, of course, even the very limited Irish war, always kills the innocent. And after all, many note, the RAF in one night in Hamburg killed more German civilians than all the victims of the Irish Republican movement since 1798. No matter, IRA operations in England, directed by the foolish, the limited, and the incompetent, all but assure civilians as targets, often not as mistakes. In the Six Counties there have been operations, often independent, locally organized, but subsequently tolerated by the Army Council, against civilians—sectarian attacks against Protestants, Loyalists victims chosen by category, in retaliation, deemed guilty by location. These operations are ideologically wrong but often practically effective, if distasteful. Such targets and such operations are at the edge of IRA military toleration, which is of course no comfort to the victims.

All of these operations, military operations against a formal enemy according to the IRA, do not take place in isolation; for just as the primary uniformed, military targets blur out into secondary ones, so too are operations for the IRA focused outside the battle-zone. An army, much less a movement, has many needs and, obviously, a desire to limit the opponent's resources as well. There are many battle arenas, some violent, most not. Prisons, for example, have always been an IRA contact point, an opportunity to serve the movement as well as the imposed sentence. Here the uncertain volunteers are further politicized and trained; here the authorities are confronted, challenged; here the interned contribute, even dominating the struggle during the hunger strikes. But in prison they are hardly noticed most of the time unless there is an escape.

The more obvious arena is that of politics, an extension of the armed struggle by other means, by all the conventional avenues of legitimate activity buttressed by the availability of unsanctioned means—theft, intimidation, violence, armed force. In politics also the IRA may have targets vulnerable to physical force. Certainly, this is the case in raising money and acquiring arms, in marshalling needed resources, ideally from the enemy—but in the current campaign mostly from friendly sources. Thus, an arms raid or an armed robbery, the extortion of contributions, the theft of ammunition are an integral part of any revolutionary organization's operations manual—indicate resource-targets. And like any large organization the movement operates on good intelligence funneled through specific assigned commanders; intelligence sought and often found by illicit means. The movement also requires the skills of diplomacy but not so often as to assign many to the task easily handled by few. This is not the case with publicity, an arena almost as vital as politics and which, like politics, has generated its own momentum within the Republican movement. Many of the movement's activities, then, lie outside the purely military and involve targets not amenable to force. Such force is, however, always available if the target is vulnerable, tempting, and ideology amenable. The key target may remain "the" enemy; but an armed campaign also focuses on things, things needed, things that can be denied an enemy, targets that arise from the demands of the periphery, from the movement as a whole—and of course some resource targets are simply military targets as well.

Active underground armies thus require extensive resources that cannot readily be found among their own: arms, especially technologically advanced arms, communications equipment, gear of all sorts from cars to chemicals, and money, always more money, arms and money, money and arms, are the key. A secret army requires all those everyday things that real armies tend to take for granted: beds and doctors and meals, telephones and printers, not to mention internal welfare payments, travel allowances, pensions and rewards. Much of this can, if matters go well, be supplied from within the Republican movement, from friends and from neighbours unknown to the security forces, from the American diaspora, from sources beyond easy reach of the police or army or the television teams. Funds are given or earned within a black economy, houses and farms are lent, services offered, computer time found—all near enough to legal not to be disruptive. Some resources, however, cannot be bought legally, borrowed from friends, or collected by a quick whiparound.

Arms are stolen on raids or acquired in illicit and often violent operations. Although arms supplies fall outside military targeting in many cases, the IRA has always been willing to mount operations that will result in an increased armory. Shipments from America, purchases on the continent, and arrangements in the Middle East have largely been responsible for arming the IRA—arms raids are rare, theft is no longer as necessary. In fact, by 1989, although still without ground-to-air missiles and with a declining amount of sophisticated explosives, the IRA had more arms than active service volunteers, more

AK-47s that could possibly be used. IRA arms, in any case, are used over and over until captured, the same weapon often moved about the province as needed.

What no underground ever has more of than is needed is money. The basic IRA needs are regularly supplied by internal sources, dues and donations and the black economy. Often sudden campaigns like that of the hunger strikers generate the needed new funds. Spectacular operations—Thatcher or Mountbattan—encourage the support groups. Money is particularly necessary during quiet periods, like that since 1987. Then expensive operations must be mounted with no sure return in publicity—money tomorrow when money is wanted today. An opportunity to purchase advanced time fuses or Italian sub-machine guns is fleeting and money required immediately. The Army Council over the years has spent considerable time on fiscal matters. Yet the IRA always seems to scrape through, collects the necessaries, often avoids the need to authorize dangerous operations, especially in the Twenty-Six Counties; but it is a long-lived problem. And for revolutionary movements if it is *not* a problem, if the group has too much money, too many guns, other and more serious troubles are certain to arise. The IRA, however, has never faced these troubles: money is always needed, more today than yesterday.

When conventional financing fails, the IRA, as have others, resorts to revolutionary expropriation: the technical term for armed robbery or extortion. Stalin was a bank robber and so have been a remarkable number of idealists: stealing weakens the institutions of the state and funds the revolution. This is fine in theory but less so in practice to volunteers who have joined an army, not a robber-gang. The feeling in Provo circles was that this was what Saor Éire was, what the Official IRA became, and what Costello risked with the INLA. Still, the IRA has seldom hesitated to rob the state—in particular post offices and banks—and other Six-County targets, even those not easily rationalized and, if pressed, extend operations to the Twenty-Six Counties: All-Ireland theft. Contributions are accepted that any observer would agree are less than voluntary and services supplied at no cost. There is often considerable leeway in these operations in Northern Ireland, but less so in the South where there are—supposedly—restrictions on military operations, restrictions that need not prevent kidnapping for ransom and the robbery of the mails or the killing that may arise thereby. The Provos are often a bit uneasy about such targets but the same was not true for the INLA. Costello had fewer scrumples and more pressing needs. The secret unOfficial IRA, the few old gunmen at GHQ felt that the comrades in Ireland needed the money more than the state or the banks. Unease has never aborted a needed Provo operation.

The time that the Provos are most likely to seek fiscal targets is during the doldrums when an opportunity to acquire gear occurs or simply when the regular bills come due with no funds left in the kitty Mostly the Army Council would prefer to avoid the inevitable fall-out of bank robberies, kidnappings, hostage negotiations, all the criminal connotations a revolutionary movement seeking legitimacy always wants to avoid. Freelance adventurers have been less image conscious—opting for the spectacular. Thus the IRA leadership discovers that a hostage has been taken without authorization or that a collection of paintings has been stolen—without anyone in the IRA the wiser until the pictures turn up in a safe house. Volunteers are inclined to see their opportunities and take them without rationalization or permission from the center. Just as Loyalist paramilitaries, or even just everyday Protestants, have been shot in spite of policy without orders, or English civilian targets picked despite policy without orders, so too in money matters the dream is bypassed because of need. And an underground always needs money and can rarely return ideologically improper spoils. Money matters, even and particularly to dreamers, and so is always a valid target.

In targeting there are, unlikely as it often seems to the conventional opponent, all sorts of *eschewed* targets, those formally denied by culture, wont, experience and ideology and those never considered, beyond contemplation—immoral, counter-productive, so unappealing as not even to be considered by those in control. Even with most non-targets there are exceptions. The IRA is not inclined to kill clergymen, unless in British uniform, innocent women or children, unless by error, the police or army in the Republic, unless necessary. Tit-for-tat killings of Protestants are prohibited before they occur but often not afterwards; for the IRA center understands the motive, the necessity, and may fear discipline will produce schism There nevertheless exists in effect—and often in reality—forbidden ground, perhaps never crossed, never even considered: the assassination of charismatic religious leaders, lady members of the royal family, Southern politicians, no matter how anti-Republican. No plane has been hijacked—but helicopters, boats and buses have. Many terror operations are quite within the capacity and imagination of the IRA but not on the cards. The same people who sent bombers to Britain were horrified by the Lod massacre by the Japanese Red Army and the Italian *Brigate rosse* Euro-terror.

Some operations are obviously so counterproductive to IRA aims as to be ignored by consensus: armed force within America, where the Irish diaspora is doubly patriotic and the authorities sufficiently difficult without provocation. Others, so simple to propose by analysts, are beyond the imagination and capacity of the center always on the run with limited resources, with many requests, with little time for contemplation, for proper prior planning, for speculation and innovation. What would appear, even given the limitations, quite possible, does not appear so when even keeping the active service people on the run, the organization ticking over, and the present campaign going is an enormous struggle, often in doubt. The covert world of the IRA is inefficient, demanding, dangerous, no place for elaborate plots or operations more suitable for thriller plots and articles in scholarly books on hi-tech terror. Anthrax and arsenic are alien; an IRA nuclear device is ludicrous. Always the old ways seem more promising, minor adjustments, slight shifts sufficient unless the skills and technological advances, IRA or British, make obsolete the congenial means and so impose new directions, a new hunt for softer targets or untouched options.

Beyond specific Republican ideological restrictions, the limitations imposed by lack of time and resources, the counter-productive and the immoral, there are operations that simply do not occur to the IRA or operations that would appear dangerous to the image of an Irish liberation movement. Thus an enormous amount of effort has been spent on operations to acquire ground-to-air missiles, an appropriate military asset, but quite literally no serious thought to biological warfare, gas or poison, much less radiation. And even the hi-tech nodes in post-western societies, the keys of command and control run by computers, the technological links, the records on silicon chips, the control of air traffic, all the targets of the theorists, have been beyond serious consideration.

Thus, while a few targets are considered and rejected for varying reasons, many targets are not considered at all—a negative consensus exists because the idea is wrong for the movement or the means are too complex to raise interest. While the IRA often has good operational skills, the organization lacks native hi-tech skills or access to congenial experts. One effort was made to construct missiles in America. Some options are passingly contemplated—hijacking on sea or in the air—but without serious action. Sometimes, however, the eschewed list is reduced, but more often because the existing list of targets has been narrowed by British skill rather than because the Army Council or the local commanders are opposed to novelty. Spreading out the old targets has long been a possibility, so that bombs are moved into England and gunmen appear in Gibraltar or Holland:

same tactics, similar targets, different arena.

There are also operations that in a conventional sense do not have an overt military component but which have led to violence: created unanticipated targets. Efforts by GHQ to arm the IRA have produced a remarkable litany of failures, several crucial key shipments, not all from the Middle East, and a tale of spectacular adventures; but there has been little violence and hence no targets in an everyday sense. Any peripheral violence, a riot at a funeral or a shootout at the end of a demonstration, is usually easily subsumed into normal campaign categories even if it was quite unexpected.

These occurrences, often focused on resources both real and symbolic, are in many cases vital to the armed struggle, even if not military. Many of the "targets" of the movement, some crucial, still require similar selection, command and control, discipline, dedication, allocation of resources, and at the end lessons to be learned. Prison escapes, whether organized almost entirely from the outside, like the helicopter descent that snatched Seamus Twomey, Kevin Mallon and J. B. O'Hagen from the Mountjoy Prison yard on October 31, 1974, on the fourth attempt, or from the inside like the great Maze escape of September 25, 1983 when thirty-eight IRA prisoners broke free and nineteen of these stayed out, have military components. According to Republican rules, escapes are a real "target" since service in prison is no less important than service outside. The prison problems involving escape, resistance, politicization and training, special intelligence and regular communication have at times all but dominated the armed struggle. Then, too, politics in and out of Sinn Féin, not only the conventional electoral, clientelist aspects but also the exploitation of issues, the attacks on real and symbolic enemies, the requirements of security and intelligence, all present the movement with targets integral to the armed struggle. Stretching over all is the vital problem of money: funds acquired legally and openly, those expropriated or donated illicitly, the problems of transit, deposit, storage and fair allocation. This produces military targets as well as the need for special operations and covert intelligence chores best handled by the IRA. Any movement must maintain a diplomatic capacity—recognition and legitimacy, alignments and alliances abroad are movement targets that at times absorb military capacity. As C/S Joe Cahill spent most of his time on a diplomatic mission and other active leaders have been abroad for diplomatic purpose. And the leadership of the IRA in Ireland must often become involved in all sorts of negotiations with revolutionary colleagues, agents of influence, potential allies and declared enemies. Often such endeavors require that the gun be introduced into diplomacy, at least as protection and at times as argument.

Summary

Some IRA enemies are not easily noted as targets. Some operations engender targets—armed danger—unexpected and often unwanted. Mostly, however, IRA targets are those of any armed struggle: individual enemies in groups, in symbolic office, in action and in places, and their resources—and/or those resources necessary to persist and escalate wherever found: people and things.

IRA Targets: Case Studies

In general there is nothing complex or mysterious abut most potential IRA targets. All the security forces in the province along with their reserves, auxiliaries, surrogates, and associates from bureaucrats to construction gangs are vulnerable—a universe of, perhaps, 40,000 to 50,000 people. Many of these would be hard targets, soldiers in barracks, and many very soft, a clerk in his garden; but all would fit Provo security categories. Out from Northern Ireland would be similar categories in England (not Wales or Scotland) and the continent—and further—less vulnerable through location, not occupation. Coupled with the physical quarters and tangible security assets, the list is enormous. Even if the smallest capacity of the IRA is used, what is remarkable is that so few operations succeed or even reach the point of visibility: in part because of excellent British responses and in part because of the restrictions imposed by guerrilla-overload. An underground can only organize so many operations in a given area regardless of the wealth of resources available. So most targets are obvious and most operations fail.

The easiest operations target the soft edges—secondary individuals or isolated resources—or a novel arena where security is lax—Germany or Gibraltar. In point of fact, most of these unconventional operations are quite conventional and only grow complex when a specific and particular target is chosen, usually for symbolic reasons, like Mountbatten or Thatcher, or a very hard mark, Scotland Yard or Lisburn barracks, is selected. Most IRA operations arise from a round of constant prowling, local observation, a steady-state search for a momentary vulnerability and thus a snatched opportunity. Few are effective.

The more conventionally military these IRA operations, at least the more orthodox the target, the easier is the analysis. Every member of the British security forces, always, at home or on parade, is a target. A glance at the television coverage of the British presence in the North, army patrols in Belfast seeking cover in doorways, amid shoppers, behind prams, is ample evidence of which people are targets. Troops on the ground move on the streets and through the country fully alert, on edge for a sniper, a mine, a culvert bomb, any dangerous movement or anomaly. Troops not on duty stay out of sight behind fortified barrack walls, protected by watchtowers and patrols. And the police are little different but in the color of the uniform. These security people, the pointed end of British control, and their civilian security colleagues, are always at risk, each a target—the judge, the custom official, the infantry brick—and the IRA selection of the particular is determined by the conditions on the ground, patterns of behaviour, unanticipated vulnerabilities and luck. And anyone in any security category will do, any time, any place. British officials are prone to point out how patient the IRA volunteers are in such matters, even at times what effective terrorists they are; but, again, it is not so much patience as the fact that there are so many targets. Even then most operations abort, over and over again. Even when all the back-up for an ambush is in place, even when the opportunity exists for a single shot to be fired by one of the adequately trained marksmen, even when the way out is secure, mostly nothing happens: the British patrol changes route, no soldier is ever still long enough for a shot, children are in the way or a car or a cow, the back-up is disturbed by a man walking a dog, an RUC patrol car moves on to the next street, something. Sooner or later, however, the moment of opportunity arises, the rifle cracks, and usually, not always, a near miss occurs: hits are more to be found on the army range than off the Falls Road. And so there is always a search for easier targets, if not people, then things, in order to keep up the pressure, persist until the British will falters. This is why all targets are chosen and always the principle remains—better some target than none.

Some targets are almost purely symbolic without viable worth in a military armed struggle—monuments, statues, private homes. Militant Republicans have tended to see such as outward signs of the imperial system, as do many rebels. The destruction of a big house or an equestrian statue, especially during a lull in the action, indicates the continuing vitality of the movement, the persistence of physical force and the old ways, the need for action. The most obvious modern example was the destruction of Nelson's Pillar in O'Connell Street in Dublin in the spring of 1966—fiftieth anniversary of the 1916 Rising and an Ireland still not free—by a tiny group of independent Republicans funded by the residue of Clann na Gael in America. It is possible, however, to combine strictly military targets with those of enormous symbolic importance so that murder becomes assassination or arson symbolic. This consideration is always present and particularly displayed by the most devout physical force Republican, not so dedicated to the gun that a sign is to be denied. Thus some people and some things may be more important than others—one of the reasons that informers and heretics are such necessary targets is that they are signs of betrayal, the failure of the dream to convert and to maintain the faith.

The Individual as Target: Categories and Symbols

Once the IRA campaign moved over to the offensive in the spring of 1971, certain categories of targets remained constant. Soldiers were first at risk, then others. These new categories tended to broaden quickly and remain stable, so that volunteers soon did not even remember when units could not attack RUC reserves. The prime target, the security forces, loosely defined by the IRA Army Council, was expanded to offer more soft options. They could, can be, hit whenever and wherever vulnerable by any volunteer. At times over the past twenty years, the volunteer has done the deciding not any command structure. At times, however, a specific, often symbolic target is selected, often but not always from the top. There is no doubt that the more symbolic and special such a target the less discussion was necessary—the single gunman would have snatched such a target without authorization, without pause if the opportunity occurred. Most targets are obvious. Some people are added to the target lists to keep the options up, to keep the campaign going, to respond to shifts and changes in reality, to fill movement needs and priorities often only marginally related to damaging the opponent's will—there are all sorts of reasons to target an informer or a heretic, pragmatic, exemplary, symbolic.

The IRA has from time to time placed in vulnerability new categories of individuals—

judges or warders or construction workers—and then let such targets lapse with a decline in enthusiasm or a rise in popular protest. At times the first victim is a result of local choice, perhaps misplaced local enthusiasm, a special desire for vengeance, or a logic chain not apparent at a higher level of command. An effort at some level may have to be made to rationalize the new category. In most cases GHQ or Northern Command will accept the local reasoning; in some cases the new range of targets comes from the center. The IRA is not in the business of protecting targets unless such targets are prohibited by ideology or by common sense, a quality not always in evidence during an armed struggle. The new categories may, if logical in Republican eyes, become permanent, as has been the case with RUC reserves and Ulster Defence Regiment's part-time members—in uniform or out and in some cases in the reserve or out—the retired may be shot too. In some cases, if unpopular or counterproductive, operations taper off and the other "targets" in the category are safe for the time being. In February 1977, the local IRA shot and killed Jeffrey Agat, the head of DuPont Corporation's Derry division: "Those involved in the management of the economy serve British interests." The murder of businessmen because they were businessmen engendered the enthusiasm only of the main advocate of such targets on the GHQ and little within Republican ranks. The distance between administering a business and being an enemy of Ireland was too great for most observers and in time the campaign was quietly called off . Mostly, however, the individuals within the security categories remain targets, everywhere vulnerable.

Sniping Ambush, Derry City, March 1972

Between the introduction of internment in August 1971 and the ending of the Republican no-go zones in Belfast and Derry by the British Operation Motorman in July 1972, the Irish conflict escalated into an all but irregular war, albeit one with limiting ground-rules. The result was that the IRA commanders soon had an open season on the security forces, often vulnerable, not yet prepared for an irregular war, nowhere more so than in the urban areas. The IRA armed struggle developed considerable momentum, using a mix of locally selected means that had at one time or another been authorized or tolerated by the center—mostly encouraged by the center—car-bombs, sniping, mines, trap ambushes, shoot-outs, booby traps, and a variety of explosive devices. Local commanders were expected to keep up the pressure, their companies to mount continuous operations when possible, and, if there was a shortage of explosives for bombs, to keep shooting with recourse to riot and arson if all else failed. Many of these small operations were almost ritual, sniping as a rite of passage for nationalist men and women. This was especially true in Derry, a small city with narrowly defined nationalist areas and highly visible British posts.

After the end of the unilateral IRA truce in March, which had been briefly imposed by GHQ to indicate the control of the center over the escalating campaign, incidents in Derry increased in number even without materials for the massive bombing campaign that would come later. At one almost traditional point on the safe side of a wall, two IRA volunteers from one of the

Creggan-based companies set up an ambush simply by removing a couple of bricks. Different bricks were removed each time since the British troops, after a brief period under fire, soon located the new slot in the old wall. Both volunteers began firing, one with an old Lee-Enfield rifle that required bolt-action and some skill and the other with an M-1, semi-automatic and equally old: the new Armalites had not drifted through to Derry. Urban guerrillas learn mostly on the job, fire all their shots in anger, and so there was no surprise when the M-1 jammed. Not that the M-1 could have been very effective since the British target post was beyond its 400-yard maximum range—in fact the British target was beyond the skills of the volunteers. With British return fire pinking the wall and spraying overhead into the hill to the rear—fire both prompt and heavy for the British army had learned in military schools and camps not on the job—the two volunteers withdrew. In time skills improved—on both sides—as did weapons and techniques.

Over the years IRA ambushes, grown more sophisticated and more complex as the British filtered out vulnerablities, have taken a toll. They do find a target now and again, just as the British have imposed a certain number of IRA losses as a result of volunteer carelessness or bad luck or a new technology. It cost IRA lives to discover that British snipers could see at night. In March 1972, two IRA volunteers, seemingly protected by the dark, had been shot and killed on the Creggan estate. Such technological escalation imposed limitations on IRA operations. After 1973 the number of incidents tapered off—not only for technical reasons but also for those of policy and organization. Regardless of the level of skills and the nature of the British security response, the local IRA units continue to deploy what they have against traditional targets—often without any authorization and often without any effect. The more intense the struggle the more likely that the decision will be local, often very local—the man with the Armalite. The more difficult an ambush, the more time, effort, organization, and risk involved, the more likely the involvement of a higher level of command. And this is true if the target is in any way novel, although by 1990 the expansion of targets gave all volunteers an enormous menu of the permitted. Most items on the list escape, if not notice, at least harm. While all members of the security forces and their friends know that they may be a target, *are* a category target, fewer are ever aware that they have been, if fleetingly, a specific target. Most specific targets thus walk away untouched, often innocent that they have passed in harm's way. Those few who become victim, add to the statistics of a low-intensity conflict that only appears intense in the totals, topped up year by year, or to those who make up those totals.

The ideal target for the IRA in March 1972 was the British army and this has been the case over the entire course of the armed struggle; but soldiers are rarely vulnerable, nor are most of the security forces. To maintain pressure the IRA must seek vulnerabilities and widen target categories, move downmarket into secondary enemies. So the IRA, often before the fact, always with a rationale after the first victim, announces special categories: prison warders, recruiting personnel, construction workers engaged on rebuilding bombed police or military barracks, customs officials, judges, or associates of the military, felon setters or informers, bureaucrats and female police. A category of targets never announced and rarely admitted remains the loyalist paramilitaries who as Irish working class should not be enemies at all. To maintain a role as nationalist defender the IRA from time to time has had to authorize retaliatory operations undertaken with varying degrees of enthusiasm by local units or, worse, has had to tolerate independent revenge operations. Each time there is a decline of loyalist paramilitary militancy or an end to sectarian killings by Protestants, there is enormous IRA relief, ideological relief as well as community relief, at the center of the Republican circle. History's rules inherited from Tone have had to be bent because of contemporary reality but not with satisfaction. Those Republicans who would shoot bigots keep their enthusiasm in check. Those Republicans who would shoot only military targets have been forced to accept over time that such denial would in effect end the campaign. The result, as far as people-targets are concerned, is that for most categories the season is always open although from time to time priorities shift (campaigns against secondary security targets tend to fade away as other issues emerge) and on occasion reaction to the new soft category, for example, businessmen, is sufficiently negative to persuade the involved to let the matter slide. Some, heretics, informers, the loyalist paramilitaries, are targeted in response to individual provocation rather than as symbols or general categories—a single act usually has made them enemy, not a career choice.

Some targets always have symbolic value— each British soldier sent home in a coffin represents more than simply a single life lost. Some targets, people-targets, are both systemic and symbolic and, as targets, the more important they are in the system and the more representative of that system the more fetching as victim. To seek out and attack such individuals is not a matter of seeing an opportunity and pulling the trigger, which is often the case in an ambush: any soldier will do, hitting the colonel is luck. When it is not luck, when command and control from the center are involved then the people target has become particular, either as singularly guilty in the case of a specific informer or exceptionally symbolic as in the case of the British prime minister.

Assassination Attempt on General Sir Ian Freeland, Summer 1971

Lieutenant-General Sir Ian Henry Freeland was the first GOC (General Officer Commanding) and overall Director of Operations in Northern Ireland from the time the British Army was put on the streets of Derry and Belfast in August 1969 until he was replaced on February 4, 1971, by Lieutenant-General Erskine Crum. In point of fact, Freeland oversaw the escalation of the Provisional IRA from a tiny, band of conspirators, unable to protect their own, into an underground guerrilla army. The IRA became so formidable that the Stormont Prime Minister, Major James Chichester-Clark, announced that "Northern Ireland is at war with the Provisional IRA," when a sniper killed the first British soldier of the Troubles, Gunner Curtis, on February 6 1971, two days after the general's replacement arrived. For the Provisional IRA and much of nationalist Belfast, Freeland was remembered not so much for the British army's counterproductive anti-insurgency policies as for his public statements and his hard tactics. In fact he was considered by Irish nationalists to have been responsible for the decision to impose a three-day curfew on the lower Falls Road, Friday, July 3, to Sunday, July 5, that produced five civilian deaths with sixty others injured compared with fifteen soldiers injured. This actually was a major factor in IRA growth. Freeman was recalled ever afterwards with bitterness, in particular for a statement made on the *Panorama* television program on Monday, April 6, 1970, that hereafter those who threw petrol bombs could be shot. In Belfast in 1970, throwing petrol bombs, even if with spectacular results, was hardly considered provocative or even as dangerous as throwing stones. It was mostly a ritual and certainly not justification for murder by the army—and it was a response that would never have occurred to Freeland if the bottle had been tossed in Manchester or Notting Hill. One of those who filed away information of Freeland's retirement first from Northern Ireland and then from the army was the IRA Chief of Staff Seán MacStiofáin, who by 1971 had tight control over the still expanding organization—or as tight as Irish custom permitted. His operations officer in

London reported back that Freeland was vulnerable each Sunday when he left his parish church. Thus MacStiofáin ordered the assassination and dispatched two experienced volunteers with two brand new German revolvers. He also indicated to O/C Britain that the movement needed money as well. Fortunately for Freeland the British IRA unit tried for the money first, the operation collapsed, and one volunteer and the revolvers were lost. No further attempt was made on the target. As an exercise in concept, intelligence, command and failed control the Freeland operation was honed down to four men and one "obvious" target only vulnerable because he was retired from the primary arena.

Assassination may come through a command directly from the top, conceived by the C/S and pursued through the minimum organizational involvement: no GHQ discussion, no Army Council authorization, no local unit participation beyond the intelligence work of O/C Britain. The total active service unit involved consisted of only two experienced gunmen and two guns, a minimal investment halved by the failed bank robbery. A similar attack on General Frank Kitson, credited by the IRA as the father of British anti-insurgency doctrine, who had brought Irish practice to theory in his Northern posting, was also considered by MacStiofáin. In point of fact neither Kitson nor his work on low-intensity operations was well received by his own when he served in Ireland for two years, 1970-1972, although later his conclusions—"...what everyone had always known..."—did become practice. No matter, the Irish in general and the radicals in Britain in particular made Kitson symbol of oppression and military manipulation. Thus when he left to command the school of infantry at Warminster, Wiltsire, his symbolic value remained high. MacStiofáin, however, had no time but to consider the prospects over the six weeks before he was arrested in November 1972. Since MacStiofáin spoke with none of those who replaced him at the center, the Kitson target disappeared from view. To be attractive, symbolic targets must retain a high visibility—once a prime minister always a prime minister—or simply be highly visible.

Assassination Attempt on John Taylor, Unionist MP on Friday, February 25, 1972, in Armagh

In 1972 John Taylor, MP for South Tyrone, young, articulate, scathing, was taken by many in Ireland as the unpleasant face of militant Unionism: unrepentant, arrogant and assured, he was unfairly blamed in considerable part for the introduction of internment in August 1971 when he was Parliamentary Secretary in the Stormont Home Ministery. The Provos GHQ had already considered him as a potential target, along with William Faulkner, who had taken over from Chichester-Clark as Stormont Prime Minister in March 1971, and the usual target-spectrum of less notorious officials in customs or the post or on the bench. The Official IRA GHQ had no such interests, no target list and no real military strategy other than a generalized disapproval of whatever their Republican Provisional IRA rivals were doing. This was not necessarily the case with the local IRA commanders, eager to act in an appropriate way—no bombs but political targets.

The Official IRA commander in the Armagh area felt that Taylor was an obvious target, the more so since he led a normal life without the use of heavy security. In Armagh town he parked his car regularly in the same spot and took no precautions—after all the Republicans had not then made an attempt on any Northern politicians. In fact both the Provos and Officials tended to avoid what might be considered sectarian targets—Harland and Wolff or Mackie's, businesses as always dominated by a Protestant workforce, Orange meeting halls, much less Protestant churches, or Protestant pubs, even those notorious as seats of Orange mobs. In the early spring of 1972, it was still not apparent that the Orange militants, with or without proper Unionist support, were involved in a murder campaign; but it was all too clear that John Taylor represented the establishment detested by all nationalists and did so with pride and manifest superiority. Thus the Officials in Armagh mounted an assassination attempt. On the evening of February 25, Taylor left his father's office at 5.30, went around the corner and got into his car. Almost immediately an IRA volunteer opened up with a Thompson sub-machine-gun, riddling the car with seventeen bullets and hitting Taylor seven times, five times in his head and jaw. At first Taylor thought he had been bombed—the noise was horrendous—but he felt no pain. He was rushed to Armagh City Hospital where amazingly he could be listed as "ill but out of immediate danger." The Official IRA Northern Command took responsibility. GHQ in Dublin first learned of the operation on the news. The general response in Dublin was that Taylor was an appropriate target, that the commander in Armagh had acted properly, and the only complaint was that somehow the victim had escaped. After the débâcle at Aldershot when only innocents were hurt, it was a relief that an operation had gone reasonably well even if the victim had escaped: at least a point had been made.

There was thus a considerable residue of militancy at the center of the Official IRA even if the currents were running in another direction. GHQ could not simply close down the campaign nor did it want to do so in February 1972. GHQ would have preferred more political options and certainly, once Stormont was promulgated in March 1972, fewer military adventures; but there was still the draw of the army, the competition with the Provos, and the rules of the past. There were, then, no GHQ lessons to be learned from the Taylor assassination attempt except that in February 1972 the gun still had a place in Irish politics—in time, for those in the center in Dublin, that place would grow small, have only a subsidiary role in finance and security. Within a very, very brief time, the gun forgotten, any armed struggle was anathema to the Workers Party and that of their former Republican rivals the Provisional IRA wicked, evil, a violation of class principles and the tenants of scientific socialism: none so vindictive as a reformed gunman. The Provos, soon after 1972 *the* IRA, had no qualms about their armed struggle or targets like Taylor, who had been on their target list.

—

Assassination of Ambassador Christopher Ewart-Biggs, July 21, 1976, Dublin

For most ambassadors, including the British, a Dublin posting was a comfortable sinecure with few problems and almost no policy input required. For exampe, in April 1970, after postings in Senegal and Mauritania, Strasbourg and the Foreign Office, Sir John Peck arrived in Dublin to live, largely unnoticed, through the dramatic early years of the Troubles. Delighted with Dublin, he retired to Dun Laoghaire outside the city at the end of his career in February 1972: no symbol of Perfidious Albion. In 1976 the newest British ambassador, Christopher Ewart-Biggs, was less low-key if no less genial, a striking figure with a smoked glass monocle, author of thrillers banned by the Irish censor—not for their political content—and who had seen service in various significant posts during troubled times. He had been threatened by the OAS in Algeria. The Irish newspapers tended to treat him as a cross between Bertie Wooster and Colonel Blimp although among his colleagues he was thought to have an acute mind. He was certainly well briefed on Irish matters and boded fair to be a substantive rather than social representative. As a matter of course the GHQ I/O was directed to check out the new ambassador by Seamus Twomey, C/S, and by the Army Council; in 1972 the IRA was still centered in and about Dublin. The I/O report was that Ewart-Biggs had been involved in British intelligence and was going to be a key player. Most important, his security, while real, was not solid—after all he was in Dublin, not Belfast. The IRA's Army Order No 8 that prohibited military action against the state in the South could, GHQ felt, be interpreted broadly to permit an operation against the British ambassador: Army Order No. 8 was almost always interpreted to permit in the South what the center wanted to do in the South. A Special Operations Unit was created, composed of volunteers available from Dublin, Dundalk and Belfast.

On July 21, the IRA unit detonated a road-mine as the Ambassador's 4.2 litre Jaguar limousine was only a few hundred yards from the residence; Irish security was not present at all times. The watching IRA volunteers, armed with carbines and garands, withdrew without firing once they saw that the Jaguar had been blown over on its left side in a smoking crater. The escort car could do nothing. Ewart-Biggs was dead. His companion, Brian Cubban, Permanent Under-Secretary of the Northern Ireland Office, was injured, and his secretary, Judith Cooke, killed. The chauffeur, Brian O'Driscoll, was also injured but he, like Cubban, recovered. The Irish police never found the volunteers nor very many valid clues. The Army Council, GHQ and the IRA felt that the operation, although in the South, was exemplary. Their Republican constituency agreed, even though there was general horror in Ireland and abroad at the murder. It was seen as an atrocity, an act of terror against a diplomat, a brilliant and witty man with an attractive wife and family, an innocent. The IRA was unrepentant in public and in private: Ewart-Biggs was a proper target, a key component of the British war machine in Ireland.

Assassination of Lord Mountbatten, August 27, 1979, Mullaghmore, County Sligo

By 1979, the IRA armed struggle was in the doldrums, a long, low-intensity war of attrition, set back, many Republicans felt, by the relatively one-sided truce accepted by the Army Council. The IRA seemed without immediate prospects. But for some months a spectacular operation had been in the works—not for the first time—with a target that guaranteed impact. For years Lord Mountbatten, various members of his family, and some of his friends had vacations at Classiebawn Castle near Mullaghmore in County Sligo, not far in miles from the bandit country of Northern Ireland but seemingly in a tranquil and serene backwater. Mountbatten was received with courtesy there in Mullaghmore and the local natives hardly seemed restless. His presence was, of course, known far beyond Sligo and from the first was noted in Republican circles. As early as 1969, with nationalists fleeing the North, Republicans in the country like Ruairí Ó Brádaigh had broached the idea of seizing the house as refuge. But nothing was done: the movement had sufficient problems without becoming involved with Sligo. As the Provisional IRA moved forward in its strategy to transform its role as nationalist defender into that of a guerrilla army, the local area IRA suggested Mountbatten as a target to GHQ. In 1970 MacStiofáin as C/S turned the project down; again other priorities had to be met. Local I/Os kept a watch on Mountbatten's presence in particular. Seamus Twomey replaced Joe Cahill, arrested on the *Claudia* on March 28, 1973, as Chief of Staff and was often on the move in Monaghan. He first learned that Mountbatten was being watched each August during his Irish vacation. The O/C of the Donegal IRA was keen on the prospect of Mountbatten as target, but had not been able to find any vulnerability. Finally in 1976 serious steps were taken to implement the operation, but first the truce and then local difficulties hampered any progress. With the truce at an end, there was excellent local information and a new determination, so much so that British intelligence picked up rumors that Mountbatten was on an IRA target list but neither warned him nor increased his security. Some British intelligence people felt that having a royal as a target would be a dramatic change in IRA policy, but if the information arose from real IRA sources (written IRA Army Council target lists distributed within the organization are rare, if discussion of targets less so), the British should not have been surprised. The IRA has, sensibly, always had an interest in high visiblity targets but seldom the capacity or the intelligence to proceed. In Mountbatten's case the vulnerability was his boat, *Shadow V,* unguarded at night—knowledge of which fact did not need the intimate inside IRA source that British intelligence later suspected.

The operation was quite small, handled by Tommy McMahon, a carpenter from Carrickmacross, who was arrested on suspicion by an Irish police patrol on August 27, even before authorities knew of the assassination. The remote-control device set off the explosives hidden on the boat at 11.30 on Monday morning. It was nearly the last 1979 chance possible. There could be no line-of-sight control because of the risks of discovery so all passengers on the

Shadow V were equally vulnerable. Mountbatten was killed, his grandson Nicholas and Paul Maxwell, a helper from Enniskillen, were also killed. Lady Brabourne, mother-in-law to the Earl's daughter, was mortally injured, while Lord and Lady Brabourne were seriously hurt. The murder of a seventy-nine-year-old royal, a national hero, a great and distinguished Englishman long retired from war and politics, devastated the United Kingdom.

Mountbatten's death swept away all other news—even the murder of old women and young boys—and was only compounded by the lost of eighteen soldiers at Narrow Water near Warrenpoint on the same day. Every English newspaper cleared the front page for Mountbatten. The entire spectrum of British opinion was horrified and condemned the killing. The same was apparently true in Ireland where authorities were appalled and the influential outraged that Ireland and the Irish would be blamed. The IRA felt justified. August 27 was the best day ever: one royal and eighteen soldiers at minimal cost; and the innocent lives were quickly ignored or forgotten in the focus on Earl Mountbatten and then the dead soldiers. Ireland and the IRA were back in the news. The cost of the long war to Britain had been stressed. The operation was judged an enormous success by the IRA leadership, by the Republican movement, by Noraid and the friends in the diaspora who received increased contributions, and by many who did not love English royals or value London's indignation. If there were a lesson to be learned it was that the Army Council grasped the enormous value of prestige targets and of the manipulation of the perceptions of the enemy, and perhaps the value of the low cost of assassination. Certainly, a first response to the hunger strike deaths in 1981 was a request by the IRA Army Council for information and intelligence on Margaret Thatcher.

Some of the more obvious targets, charismatic, symbolic, inherently dangerous, aroused little general enthusiasm because the victim was an apostate or an informer. No serious and reasonable Republican enjoys schisms and feuds—and all revolutionary movements are subject to schisms and feuds, inherent aspects of the covert world. It requires, normally, an act of will to generate enthusiasm for vengeance, although once the rounds of murder begin no feud is more bitter than that between the former faithful. Extended and emotional rationalizations are at first needed to embark on such a killing ideological quarrel—the target must be transformed from a former colleague, a fellow believer, into a wicked and evil man. And so treated, of course, he will act in turn against his wicked and evil enemies. Thus internecine quarrels become difficult to stop, impossible to control, end in absolute victory or mutual exhaustion in many cases. This is not necessarily always so, and in Ireland, where the lessons of the bitter civil strife of 1922-1923 remained fresh, most Republicans wanted to avoid a round of tit-for-tat killings. Killing symbols of British imperialism was one thing. Killing each other was another. Thus when schism led to the gun as it did first with the Officials and Provos as rival

IRAs and again between the Officials and the INLA over the second split in the orthodox ranks, many sought truce, not killing. Still the Officials, in the midst of the transformation from Sinn Féin to the Workers Party found the gun, as they had in the murder attempt on Taylor, not so easy to put on the shelf nor even to use properly once old skills and interests had eroded.

The Assassination of Seamus Costello, October 1977

There was little doubt that Costello was the dominant figure in both the IRSP and INLA, organizations at first composed of his friends and allies within the Officials and always dominated by his personality and predilections. He was capable of generating fierce loyalty and ambivalence among old associates; some could never quite trust him and others, at times, had found him indispensable. In the case of the Official-INLA 1975 feud, the feeling within the Dublin IRA GHQ was that without Costello there would be no INLA and no feud, that shooting the INLA gunnies instead of their leader was pointless. Thus GHQ targeted Costello, despite and because of past association. And to no avail. The INLA people proved deadly and resilient. Among others, the Officials lost Billy McMillen, their Belfast O/C, killed on April 28. Then Seán Garland survived an attack in Dublin on March 1 in which he was shot six times. A variety of stratagems were used to lure Costello into an ambush meeting. He never showed up. The closest the Officials came was an attempt after an IRSP meeting in Waterford on May 7. His movements were traced, his car followed by a pair on a motorbike. One of the Official Volunteers machine-gunned the car. One bullet tore a hole out of the center of the tax disc on the front windscreen but missed its target. Costello drove on to Dublin and the feud continued. With no easy end in sight, both sides agreed to a truce that, though fragile, held, since the Officials were trying to ease out of the gun business while the INLA had felt the aggrieved party whose survival the truce ensured.

The only ones disappointed were a few hard gunmen determined on vengeance, not so much from policy as from personal preference. One of these was Jim Flynn from South Armagh, who had been used by the Official IRA GHQ staff when a hard man was needed but used reluctantly since he was difficult to control and sought opportunities for violence. GHQ was in fact no more than a title given the old IRA men— Garland, who replaced Goulding as C/S in 1975, Mick Ryan and a few others clumped at the center of Official Sinn Féin. Their enthusiasm for the gun in politics varied from time to time. Ryan, perhaps the most military, believed in a role for a secret army. Over the years, primary responsibility for the military would be shifted to Mick Ryan as the long-serving director of operations. His views on the national question and the virtues of the IRA remained more traditional than those of his GHQ colleagues who were intent on political matters. Violence, the gun, the Flynns were on the way out, but not so quickly that GHQ went pacifist. For Flynn at least, eager to make a reputation, determined to be famous, a source of ballads, a name in history, action was crucial. Time was passing and his skills were not in demand. He became convinced that by eliminating Costello, a charismatic and notorious figure, his own fame would be assured. In 1977 he asked GHQ for permission to shoot Costello. Ryan and the others refused—an end to the truce would be politically insane. Flynn was persistent and his fixation general knowledge within the Officials. On October 5, Flynn, using a double-barrel shotgun, killed Costello while he sat in his car as usual on Northbrook Avenue off the North Circular Road in Dublin. That day Costello had no bodyguard with him nor any reason to anticipate an attack: the British were off in the North and the Officials into politics. Flynn made sure that those who mattered knew that the killing was his work and was Official work—he claimed permission from Cathal Goulding himself, "...a wink and a nod." Some of Flynn's associates noted that in a very similar maneuver Goulding, not the IRA GHQ, had "sanctioned" the murder of Larry White in Cork on June 10, 1975. White was one of the few members of Saoirse Éire, a splinter of the tiny Saor Éire that then dissolved on June 27 "in the interest of the working class." For a sly gunman like Flynn, aware of the White example, Goulding could have been his man, could give an imprimatur to his deed. The assassination of Costello would be Official if unofficial. Flynn appeared at GHQ immediately after the shooting and the Officials got rid of the shotgun and moved him out of the Republic into South Armagh. His fame was short-lived, however, since he talked and the word of his responsibility spread quickly. The INLA people killed him not too long before some of the Officials would have decided that he must go. Flynn was a danger to everyone, a ticking bomb. The Officials attended the funeral, paid £5,000 for a monument, but gave no oration. A violent, undisciplined, psychopath who boasted in the wrong places, talked to the wrong people, threatened those with the means to retaliate, Flynn had been living on borrowed time once he fired through the car window in Northbrook Avenue. That he managed to reach that point and was then passed through the hands of the movement indicates the decay in IRA command and control during a transition period: GHQ control was loose, found Flynn a convenience but did not adequately control him. Garland and the others had discarded some of the center's control with the old forms and priorities. Flynn, ruthless and shrewd, exploited the mix at GHQ to make formal a murder that would, as it did, assure him a footnote in Irish history. GHQ was left to pick up the pieces and move, not towards greater control but towards greater secrecy and less violence.

It is inordinately difficult to control certain hard men who can kill close up and personally without fear or remorse, a useful talent that can rarely be found in the simple soldier or the everyday volunteer no matter how brave or dedicated. Such gunmen can only be directed by one equally ruthless through fear and example, and probably never directed effectively for very long. Regardless of the reins, they tend to grow fond of their work and thus too dangerous for their commanders' intentions. The INLA killers simply pre-empted the Officials who recognized that in order to get out of the killing business they would have to kill the killers. In the long pause between the Officials' secret military actions after the truce in May 1972 and the final shift to expropriation and the defense of black economic interests (the gun as a means of funding), GHQ often failed to function properly, failed to make clear, then and later, the role of force in politics and so allowed the forceful like Flynn to pursue his targets, not theirs.

All very small revolutionary organizations can be endangered by a single malignant personality, by one mistake in targeting. In the North the loyalists were repeatedly contaminated by psychopathic killers, drunken murderers, and limited and foolish vigilantes who dominated the paramilitary organizations, who used self-awarded titles and uniforms to cover unsavory murders. The Northern vigilante experience was not unique but merely indicative of the enormous risks of the introduction of the gun into politics by those without legitimacy, without even the control of the gunmen. The IRA in its major manifestations has always claimed a historic legitimacy, has always sought to impose control from the center. The Officials, however, as they moved away from their past gave up the pretensions of orthodox Republican legitimacy for the aspirations of Marxist-Leninist radicalism. Ryan and the few militarists were gradually shunted aside. In time he left for the United States and the unofficial IRA grew more nearly "criminal." To the police and to many Irish Republicans, a bank robbery with the take divided between the perpetrators and the party is robbery-by-hire, not revolutionary expropriation. After all, even Stalin kept all his bank take for the party. And so GHQ, the few at the center of the secret, no longer functioned properly or militarily by the eighties.

Resources as Target: Destruction and Acquisition

For the innocent eyes the most noticeable result of the long IRA campaign in Northern Ireland has always been heaped rubble—which is often, in reality, the result of urban renewal, the construction of motorways or the decay of the inner city. Bombs are photogenic. Flaming buildings tended to make the evening colour television news. Some targets repeatedly attacked like the Europa Hotel in Belfast become notorious – "most bombed." Some targets are costly to replace, drain resources from the enemy; and others are irreplaceable or if sturdy highly symbolic like the Tower of London. From 1970 the Provisional IRA made use of bombs to cause damage, to inflict costs, to create turmoil and confusion, to involve the security forces, and to encourage their own. INLA and Saor Éire had no bombing resources and the Officials decided that bombing was indiscriminate, sectarian, and unlikely to lead to the specific radical political advances needed. The Provos continued, bombed away the centre of most Northern towns, extending their target list to nearly any structure not demonstrably nationalist—and even then Catholic ownership did not save designated buildings if they fit the existing target category. The poor were largely immune—the Protestants as well—for bombing inside their ghettos would be sectarian as well as dangerous. And the private homes of the rich were also ignored as being less attractive than commercial targets. So the slums and suburbs were safe. Mostly, especially in the early years, 1971-1972, the IRA concentrated on the city centers and later moved out to damage the tourist industry or bars catering to the British army or even the main streets of very small towns. Some of these category targets like La Mon, a catering facility used for a dogshow, turned disaster. All "economic" targets held an inherent risk of civilian casualties, the more so when the bombers were ill-trained, feckless and hasty. The Army Council and GHQ, cautions aside, were willing to take risks with the lives of both volunteers and civilians, given the seemingly enormous returns. By the middle of 1972, Northern Ireland looked like a war zone and was so perceived by the international media, the armed participants, and many in Britain.

Derry Car-bombs, March 21, 1972

During 1972 the IRA bombing attack on "the artificial economy" of the Six Counties devastated most of the towns and cities. There was an enormous flow of explosives, often quite primitive, and timers, often quite primitive, into the North. One of the more effective means of placement was to load a stolen car with the bulky bombs, drive to an appropriate location, usually downtown, and park at about the time a warning had been telephoned to the police using the proper codeword. The operations, like sniping, would evolve for a time into a ritual affair, but one that always threatened civilians and IRA volunteers. The explosives were not stable at times. The bomb makers had learned on the job. The detonators and timers were not perfect. Telephone-call warnings were not foolproof. The innocent were not always careful. (Windows filled with people looking down at a roped-off car-bomb ticking away boggle the mind of the cautious and wary, and the same is true for those who gather at the end of the road pushing up to see the explosions).

On Tuesday, March 21, 1972, the Derry IRA unit was organized to set several car-bombs with explosives that had been expected for several days but had only brought across the border the previous day. The heavy bags of low-grade lifting explosives refined from fertilizer were wrestled into two stolen hatch-back cars—Fords were a local IRA favourite—in a lane near the Bogside. The detonators and timing devices were slipped into the tops of the plastic bags with a circle of gelignite sticks and the results covered with old carpet. The cars were then driven to pre-selected sites while the warning calls were made from a nearby public phone. The exact placement of the car on Shipquay Street within the old city walls was dependent, as was often the case, on parking slots rather than a precise and highly symbolic target citing: anywhere along the street would do. All the bombs that day detonated as planned, the warning was effective—although a few eager watchers were sprayed with glass—and considerable damage was done to nearby stores, doing the economy no good and ensuring that the British government would face insurance claims. Over the years of the Troubles, such "economic" targets have been so general as to defy precise categories: any street will do, any site except housing estates or nationalist symbols. In Britain there are so many symbolic targets available—the Carlton Club, the Stock Exchange, posh restaurants, Harrods and the Hilton in London alone—that choice is often arbitrarily made by the one or two active service units involved. In the North the local unit's choice rests on vulnerability, the campaign pace, on the availability of explosives and, from time to time, on the instructions of either the local staff or of GHQ. Increasingly, because of British countermeasures, car-bombing, bombing in general, had to be undertaken with more care; but the targets hardly shifted except during specific series attacks against certain facilities like hotels or symbols like vulnerable government buildings. The entire process was local, often very local, except for blitz days or the onset of a truce. In recent years, then, operations have been individual—a single giant car-bomb in the middle of Belfast—instead of serial: a few specific bombs ordered from above rather than the constant din of 1972 with all the Northern IRA using up explosives as fast as they became available.

In 1972, however, bombing was a constant and the car-bomb the medium that carried the message.

Bloody Friday, the Belfast Bomb Blitz, July 21, 1972

The first car-bomb in Belfast had been ordered by the Brigade's O/C Seamus Twomey to dispose of the blackpowder shipped north from Dublin by

Jack McCabe, GHQ QMG who had established an explosives factory in his garage and would be killed by an explosion in his haste to supply the North. The first car-bomb was not considered tactically significant nor were the 1970 IRA Brigade bombs which were detonated without a Republican spokesman accepting responsibility. These operations had been authorized after General Freeland imposed the Falls Curfew, from Friday, 10:15 p.m, July 3, to Sunday, 9:00 a.m, July 5. Belfast IRA set up a special bombing squad that then detonated at least seven bombs. Not all IRA explosions were limited to Belfast but only on September 1, 1970, when volunteer Michael Kane was killed in Belfast by his own bomb, did the IRA begin to take responsibility for the bombing. It was not until much later, in 1972, that the more sophisticated car-bombs came into general use.

By summer 1972, the centers of many Northern towns and cities had been blitzed by car-bombs driven out of safe areas or no-go zones. When the short truce that followed the meeting of IRA representatives and members of the British cabinet in London on July 7 collapsed during a confrontation with the British Army on Lenadoon Avenue in Belfast on July 9, it was natural for MacStiofáin and the IRA to respond with a bomb blitz to show the cost of further war. As O/C of Belfast, Seamus Twomey informed his staff on Thursday, July 20, that a special effort from the Army Council was needed the next day. Thus on Friday, July 21, Belfast brigade detonated with warnings twenty-two bombs, many in cars, while fourteen explosions took place elsewhere throughout the North. The proliferation of warnings coupled with bad luck produced unexpected casualties: there were nine killed, including four civilians, and many injured. The IRA had simply not foreseen the difficulty that the security forces would have in clearing central Belfast and so were lumbered with the responsibility for "Bloody Friday." It was an event that gave a public rationale for the British Motorman operation to clear out the no-go zones of Belfast and Derry and that earned the Republicans an enduring reputation for callousness in undertaking dangerous operations. It did not matter, certainly to British propagandists, that the IRA did not target civilians. (The exception had been an unofficial bomb in the Abercorn restaurant on March 4, 1972, that killed two women and injured or maimed another 130 customers.) Intentional or unintentional unofficial or not, after the Belfast blitz, the IRA was for many a terrorist gang.

In time, as the war continued, the IRA did in fact permit retaliation against Protestants chosen as vulnerable, and accepted no-warning bombs during the various English campaigns, but most civilians were killed by error—as was the case on Bloody Friday—or through incompetence. The cost of such operations never outweighed the benefit as far as the active IRA was concerned. Twenty years later Republicans were still apologizing for errors. Efforts to blame the security forces for refusing to react or reacting slowly were—true or false—unconvincing except to true believers. Too many bomb targets seemed obviously to ensure great civilian risk. Was one nun "worth" the RUC constables? Within the IRA the consensus was that there was no alternative but to risk innocent lives if the armed struggle was to continue. Perfect, surgical operations so desirable in theory were usually beyond the IRA's technical capacity in practice although not always and not everywhere because some IRA unit commanders took more care, had better talent, were beneficiaries of good luck.

While almost all operations carry risk, both for the volunteers and for those near the target, some are in theory relatively clean: certain commercial targets attacked in off-hours or when surely empty, attacked when there is no prospect of guards or innocents, produce results at low cost. Unfortunately they often produce minimal results, although a massive bomb in Belfast city center detonated for midnight with ample warning given should do damage and appear in living colour on the next day's television news. Generally, the IRA, with limited technical resources, has not targeted complex systems except for a few, not always successful attempts at industrial sabotage. There is a tendency, then, to put a bomb in an underground station, a high risk to civilians, rather than close down the entire system though central sabotage. So computer systems, communication links, commercial data banks, gas pipelines and even traffic lights have escaped all but incidental damage. The most worthwhile targets are firstly in England where operations are difficult, secondly beyond reach of IRA capacities and thirdly, require unavailable technically skilled operational officers. The resource-systems that are available, vulnerable to IRA skills, and visible, often produce mixed or limited results.

The Dublin-Belfast Railway Link

On its way north from Newry the railway could hardly be satisfactorily protected. It was an ideally vulnerable resource-system given IRA capacities. From time to time local units had bombed the rails or set bombs in the passing trains without any profound operational rationale: the link, the trains were vulnerable, the British would be stretched, action was action. The southern stretch of the link in the Six Counties was easily accessible, not only to the Newry unit but also to the historic hard men of South Armagh and South Down, whose domination of their countryside, bandit country to the British—the Republic of South Armagh—had produced an almost classical rural insurgency pattern. These volunteers, who took guidance coldly, especially from the center, obviously needed no authorization to keep up the pressure. After all, South Armagh was a crucial front in the armed struggle. Much the same was true for units along the railway. In December 1988, there were two bombs in the Kilnasaggart area and the line was closed for eleven days. A "campaign" had begun, fashioned despite a growing popular distaste for cutting the railway, which was a sign of unity, not an appropriate target. The determination of the volunteers involved not to be intimidated was untouched. And at the top the Army Council with the threat of a militant Republican Sinn Féin in mind, was reluctant to penalize those volunteers involved in strikes on a heretofore legitimate IRA target. It was not a time to bow to political pressure in dealing with the IRA outside Belfast and so the bombs continued:

1989
Feb 3-21	Killnasaggart	4 bombs line closed 11 days
Feb 23-26	Lurgan	11 bombs line closed 4 days
Mar 2-8	Newry	1 bomb line closed 6 days
Apr 11-19	Newry-Dundalk	4 bombs line closed 9 days
Apr 20	Lurgan	2 bombs line closed 3 days
Jun 19-21	Finaghy	1 bomb line closed 3 days

There were also fifteen bomb scares, including eight in June, one hoax, a hijacked bus, and all traced by the authorities to the IRA. The same pattern continued throughout the summer to rising complaints. On August 2, the Northern Ireland Office minister, Richard Needham, described the bombers as "maniac" and insisted that everything would be done to keep the railway line open. Past experience should have indicated that such statements would only encourage the maniacs, who bombed for a different constituency. On August 22, an editorial in *The Irish Times* noted that bombs or scares had closed the line for fifty-seven days besides disrupting traffic for much of the time, and urged every effort to keep open the railway. For the first time in twenty years, the US State Department issued a caution to American citizens that bombs had disrupted rail service. The link was threatened not only by the IRA but also by the introduction of bus services, quite unrelated to the bombing campaign according to spokesman from Bus Eireann and Ulsterbus. Many felt that the British would be delighted to let the campaign succeed and thus have thousands blame the IRA, whose reasoning would not stand scrutiny. The rising protest, especially by the everyday people dependent on the line, led to an explanation in *An Phoblacht* on August 24 that the IRA bombs would force the British army out of its South Armagh spy post, tie down troops that otherwise would be deployed in nationalist areas, undermine British authority, and put the troops engaged in clearing the tracks at risk. "It is not our intention to close down the railway permanently—that would be self defeating." And so by September it was time to taper off the campaign before the locals alienated too many people. Protests like the Peace Train effort have little impact on Republicans, who have a different constituency and march to a different drummer. There would be further incidents in 1989-1990, as the bomb hoaxes in particular continued, but an end to the "campaign."

Many resource targets that attract attention are destroyed in the process, bombed away, burned down, ruined. It is low-intensity war at high intensity. Others, however, are not destroyed but confiscated: money, arms, information, ammunition, chemicals, houses and businesses, and always again money, which lubricates every armed struggle. The IRA as a long-lived movement generally finds little difference between these operations and the more military ones. Volunteers understand the need to acquire funds as well as to destroy department stores. Some movements, however, find it difficult to persuade a patriot to steal for his cause or to lie or to act other than as the schools have taught as honourable; other armed struggles, of course, take place in societies where cunning, cheating, and dissembling are admirable, but killing, even as a military act, may not be acceptable. Each underground must adjust to cultural imperatives. The IRA's world has persisted for so long, tolerated so much in the struggle for the Republic, that each new generation can soon slip into operational habits found necessary if unsavoury. This is not always the case: the Christian Brothers may teach patriotic history and the church may reluctantly define a just war, but, for many, the acquisition of funds, expropriation, armed robbery, much less kidnapping for gain or extortion, remain hurdles. Still, the IRA has always found those willing to extend the resource-target list to include the local post office or the mail train.

The Great Train Robbery

On March 31, 1976, at Sallins in County Kildare, the Cork-Dublin train was robbed of registered packets worth £221,000 by well-organized, well-informed, armed men in paramilitary gear. The Irish police immediately began sweeping up members of the IRSP throughout the country. Soon forty members were in jail in the first move in a dramatic and prolonged judicial crisis over the state's actions. The police were accused of faking evidence and maltreating suspects, the government in general of railroading radicals into prison, and the entire Irish judicial system of failing to produce justice. Practically the entire political and judicial community became involved, journalists produced two books and the radicals several martyrs, in particular Nicky Kelly. The defendants claimed innocence, but the government, the judiciary, the jury and a great many of the respectable did not believe them despite growing evidence to to that effect. The IRSP and the INLA, of course, claimed innocence but almost no one believed *them*. The Provos did, since they indicated in appropriate quarters that it was their operation. The Officials, now officially out of violence but all too knowledgeable about Costello and his gunmen, believed neither. They knew that Costello had taken operational plans for various armed robberies with him and had been pulling them off as fast as possible before his old comrades could do so secretly. They assumed the INLA guilty, the Provos liars.

The original idea of a Sallins robbery had occurred long before in idle IRA GHQ conversations that involved Mick Ryan, Seán Garland and a railwayman who mentioned the regular, unguarded shipment as an aside. Garland and Ryan had taken the Cork train and realized that a robbery was possible in theory. For their colleagues in 1966, a robbery was not possible in practice. Denis Foley, editor of the *United Irishman* at the time was horrified: "Over my dead body." IRA volunteers join up to fight a war, to belong to an army, not to become ideogical thieves. Every revolutionary organization tends to have the same problem: shooting is easier to teach than stealing, more military, more plausible, appropriate. Eventually in 1967 the Army Council heard of the possibility with no enthusiasm. "What if we are caught?" said Ruairí Ó Brádaigh, opposing the operation. Previous IRA operations in the forties had been counter-productive. While it was true that the movement was desperate for money, could pay no salaries, published each issue of the *United Irishman* without any security that there would be another issue, lived at times on borrowed pounds, theft did not seem a rational way out. Not to Foley or Ó Brádaigh or others. Perhaps, some time in Britain or the Six Counties but not in Dublin, not in 1967. In fact the IRA GHQ, by-passing the moralists, did carry out an armed robbery at Dublin Airport two years later, did not plan for failure, lost the money and two volunteers, each with an eight-year sentence. The constant din of the Northern crisis tended to minimize the airport scandal. The IRA involvement could not easily be proved and the GHQ organizers went untouched.

After August 1969, the defense of the nationalists required money—and lots of money began to come in from voluntary contributions, from America, and even from Irish political sources. For a rebel there is never enough money. Reluctantly the Provos in Belfast authorized the first armed robbery in 1970 and post offices and banks soon became vulnerable funding agencies for IRA expropriations throughout the Six Counties. In the South there was still some reticence: IRA Army Order No 8 (still apparently valid for both IRA groups) that, as noted, prohibited military action in the South, did not prohibit expropriations; but no one wanted to begin, yet. The money bags continued to ride up on the railroad from Cork, untouched. Along with several other obvious targets—armoured cars moving payrolls, large sums transported regularly with limited protection, small banks without guards, extremely valuable shipments trucked about without security—they were noted and discussed. The Republicans had lots of friends who were worried about the North, eager to help, less than loyal to their employer or to the state.

Saor Éire seemed interested in little else except money. Increasingly the inhibitions of the Provisional IRA decayed. The Provos undertook their first Twenty-Six-County armed robbery in August 1973 and had people on the lookout for large jobs—even in the Six Counties, nothing lower than £5,000-robberies could be authorized.[1] Costello and his lot had never had any such qualms and the unofficial Official IRA, still citing the ideological example of Joseph Stalin robbing the bank in Tiflis, moved by the people's need for money, took up theft as well.

Thus by 1976 anyone could have been guilty— the politicals or even everyday criminals—but the Provos were in fact the real perpetrators. The INLA was at work on the operation but lost out. Actually the INLA had lifted £65,000 from the wrong train in their first attempt. The Provo information on the Cork train came to an operations officer who brought the project to his contact on GHQ. The operation was shaped and brought to the Army Council that authorized a special GHQ effort: locals would not be in charge but rather a one-time active service unit. The actual Provo robbery worked easily without complications and in fact the police swoop on the IRSP people was so swift and sure that the Provos felt that such a response to the "next" Costello robbery had been pre-planned. That Costello had not done the job was then and later almost immaterial to the police—he and his

---

[1] As an aside on the control of the center, Seamus Twomey was sent to prison among other reasons for possession of £1,500 taken in a robbery in Kerry—after all GHQ could hardly return the money even if the cache was below IRA limits.

INLA *had* been doing jobs. While the Provisional C/S Seamus Twomey and the Army Council were not despondent over the fate of the INLA suspects, they did in time informally indicate that the suspects were innocent. The Officials did not believe them. The state did not choose to believe them. And so the Provos had the best of all possible worlds: the money, no guilt, no post-operations search or investigation, and credit for telling the truth that—proving their duplicity—the Officials would not accept although, gradually, everyone else did.

The Provos' train robbery indicated the importance of tight control to ensure that the deed comes within the context of an armed struggle, that the money if possible is possessed by the illegitimate establishment (the state, the banks, the bosses), that the operation will have a military cast, and, most important of all that the money does not dribble away en route to the movement coffers. At times this was the case with the INLA, when such operations in fact produced almost too much money to spend effectively. Some Latin American organizations have actually had to intimidate experts as investments advisers to disburse the vast sums arising from kidnappings, and others, like the Germans, found their volunteers driving luxury cars and living in large, elegant flats. Mostly, however, the money is gobbled up by the armed struggle, by the needs of the dependants, by election campaigns and by arms purchases. So has been the case with the Provos. The Officials, on the other hand, gave up their visible secret army and instead fashioned a small action group of twenty or so volunteers engaged in theft for the movement, a procedure ultimately corrupted and corrupting in the 1980s, the last violent vestige of the gun in politics.

The continuing problem in all operations, in particular those on the edge of revolutionary morality, is that no one plans for failure and few can anticipate the outrage and indignation arising from operational provocation. In sum, does the movement want the responsibility of authorizing theft (an armed robbery without cover of an armed struggle in a host country), a theft likely to be viewed in general as illegitimate? The same is true for every operation. Few ask, "What if?" So warnings are not phoned and the little town of Claudy is devastated by bombs so awful that the IRA would not take responsibility. So volunteers are not punished for fear of schism, and tit-for-tat sectarian murders continue. So bombs are placed in pubs or department stores without warning. So shots are fired at innocents. So a bank job in Enniscorthy in the Republic goes wrong. No one thinks ahead for there is no time nor inclination nor discipline, nor often even reward for so doing, and the penalties are patent, only when disaster strikes.

The enthusiasm of the militant and the often concomitant incompetence have over the years presented the Army Council with misguided or botched operations that, like the railway campaign, are not so much violations of history or target lists as thoughtless. No one *ever* plans for failure. No one takes into account the reaction of the innocent—empathy is rare in revolutionary circles. No one wants to consider the down side: optimism is all, action is vital and usually the local IRA operations do not gather sufficient unwanted momentum to need explanations in *An*

Phoblacht. From time to time, disasters do need to be denied or rationalized or ignored or, worst of all, call for a formal apology. Some locally chosen targets, like the railway line, like Enniskillen, like La Mon, are counter-productive. The problem for all revolutionary organizations is that there is no solution to control at the edge. Control is always too loose or too firm, whether the target is people or resources, military or symbolic. In the case of the IRA, structural permissiveness is disciplined by historic practice and present consensus: "Our rules are taken from history."

The selected case-studies are hardly tidy, do not reveal the same structured pattern in each example, are not detailed, rich in implication, analytically paralleled: and the same is true of all IRA operational data. Secret armies are secret, especially in the middle of an armed struggle. Many of those involved are still involved, still vulnerable. Many of those involved have also made an effort to forget as much as possible; many never knew the details in any case and some crucial witnesses are dead or beyond reach or recalcitrant. More important than the limited sources is the fact that those involved within the IRA center have neither the time nor the inclination to analyze the target-problem: the opportunity is recalled but not the means of the message; the decision was not "made" but was obvious; the operation was, if at all possible, isolated and cut off from the center; and any lessons learned were not from a formal debriefing or enumerated report. The IRA center was by then engaged on other matters. There is, then, in most cases no neat trail from first intelligence through authorization, command and operational control to retrospective analysis. Some operations, some targets are always on hold, always await a bit of key information—the guard is unarmed, the man goes to church every Sunday, they park behind the cinema on Friday night. Habit, ritual, patterns are automatically a matter for each and every Republic eye, some authorized as intelligence officers, most not. Just as the security forces create a vast system of deterrence to protect their own resources, all targets, so too does the IRA want all their volunteers and friends to look for potential vulnerabilities.

Some operations have long roots. Interested Republicans knew about the sacks on the Cork-Dublin train for years, watching them go by from time to time until the opportune moment after ten years of watching. Mountbatten's summer presence had been on a check-list of possibilities for a decade and had been for two years previous to 1979 the focus of a serious operation. There were ten years of vulnerability ignored by the innocent arrogance of a man who felt that a happy smile on the streets of Sligo and the kindness in the countryside, cancelled out his station and symbolic significance. He thus felt no danger only a few miles south of the killing zone, felt no need of heavy security during his summer relaxation. All the while, like the money sacks in the Cork train, he was watched, a cold target.

Other operations are swift concepts, swifty activated: MacStiofáin's choice of General Freeland, who was a natural target because of his position, because of his hard words, because of his symbolic value and unexpected vulnerability, led swiftly to action, if aborted action, once the site had been selected in England. In the case of Kitson, the target was chosen, the general location known, but time ran out for MacStiofáin and he was arrested before authorizing the operation. There are, then, always lots of targets, tens of thousands at any given moment, some more attractive to the IRA than others and some more vulnerable, but rarely both, as in the case of Thatcher and Mountbatten. Many of the targets are protected by the system and by the severe limitations imposed on IRA capacities by limited talent and extended commitments. Most targets are safe. A few targets hit spectacularly can, however, give the impression that the armed struggle is effective, escalating. Armed struggles are wars of perception so the spectacular, the impression, matters even when the butcher's bill is short, easily paid.

In analysis perception matters enormously for there is little agreement on the dynamics of the IRA. In specific operational cases the process of analysis, command and control, operational detail and reappraisal blur in reality. The IRA has never been an especially reflective organization but moves along on historic assumptions, regular practice, and occasional novelties. Everything has been done before. Everyone knows the rules, most of the limits, and the appropriate directions. Tactic consensus is the rule. The Army Council rarely votes. The operational directions rarely need debate before choice. The Chief of Staff decides or the director of Northern Command, without need of strategic planning, tactical guidelines or organizational approval. Only later can the process be picked apart from the outside to find steps and stages and factors of influence; those involved are rarely interested and later on rarely aware of the process, which is a seamless garment. Even major organizational decisions are made long before they are implemented or announced, formal closing often being postponed as long as possible to convince the last of the resistant. In 1966 it was obvious to an alien eye that the Republican movement was going to divide between the pragmatists eager to act on events through the only means—politics—and those who would prefer to wait in purity until traditional means might be deployed. It was not obvious to those involved as the center drifted on into radicalism away from physical force, and the edges hibernated. Events in the North in 1968 and 1969 simply accelerated the pace, changed no minds, but hardened hearts and replaced nostalgia with opportunity. That the gun, not their cherished politics, had a prime Northern role imposed often contorted responses on the IRA Officials, accelerating politicization, ensuring anger, arrogance, and the adamant will still found within the resulting Workers Party. The Republican movement had not so much spilt after 1969 as divided into clumps of those attracted to different poles, each labelled as the means to the future. Some Republicans have always felt that such poles are mutually exclusive. Either the core of their movement is an army or the movement has been corrupted by politicians, transformed into a party, ruined. Past experience to the contrary, some, a few, often the best and brightest and bravest, have felt that this is not the case, that politics and war are complementary, that not everyone in an armed struggle can be armed or should be. In the Officials these "military" types like Mick Ryan were edged out and in the Provos the "political" types like Gerry Adams were promoted. They have logic with them, the best arguments, contemporary revolutionary example, but not the results of the general reading of Irish Republican history, a history of confrontation, patriotism, sacrifice and failure that shimmers about the Republican grail, capable of maintaining the faith of the physical force volunteer this generation and next.

Someone like MacStiofáin with a concern for revolutionary tactics and strategy can in retirement understand the nature of target selection. If as is the wont of all retired military men he finds more order in the past than most historians would credit, many of his colleagues with other useful revolutionary virtues are not so reflective. At the center they wanted to delegate most operational matters, let others worry about tactics, and instead inject enthusiasm and mild guidance towards escalation in the evolving campaign. Some at the center had no administrative talents nor particular charisma nor novel ideas so that the Provisional IRA often seemed to move ahead on habit and past momentum through consensus—and did so far more successfully, than most revolutionary organizations could manage because history's rules were followed. All those patriot generations guaranteed IRA persistence if not escalation. In any case theorists in the center of the circle, even those with charisma and war experience like

Guevara, guarantee observer nothing but edited memories. And the IRA has never had a theorist, never much more of a strategy than seizing the opportunity to wage war as intensely as assets allow. The movement produces guerrilla manuals, not theoretical tracts. The IRA leadership always placed the movement's faith (as do all revolutionaries) in the triumph of will, the victory of history. The risen people cannot be denied:

> The IRA strategy is very clear. At some point in the future, due to the pressure of the continuing and sustained armed struggle, the will of the British government to remain in this country will be broken. That is the objective of the armed struggle.

Any target that allows the struggle to continue is tactically vital. No matter how many targets are taken—royals killed, barracks bombed, symbols destroyed, police shot and soldiers sent home in coffins, banks robbed, ships sunk, helicopters downed—the ultimate target is the will of the British, the center, the élite, the establishment and their people. In the end the numbers do not matter. The mistakes and blunders and incompetence, all of which pay some dividend, will be forgotten, the lists of dead and wounded filed, the bombed rebuilt and the insurance paid out. The armed struggle will be nothing but an aside in British history, if a new beginning in Ireland. What matters is that the British determination to persist will have been broken.

Review

Structure and Conceptions

The selection of targets is a continuing process arising from particular needs, often unarticulated, occasionally purely psychological instead of military or political, and shaped by existing organizational realities. The formal process may be important, may limit or encourage certain directions and procedures, may be an outward and visible reflection of internal order; but certainly at times the internal dynamics of the organization only marginally relate to the actual structure and announced agenda.

Thus Saor Éire, avowedly radical, deeply motivated by ideological considerations, was little more than the brief fusing of unstable ideologies and criminal opportunists, drifters eager to become involved in events when order in Ireland began to decay. The heirs of the INLA, neither ideologically motivated nor, except in rare cases, simple criminals, had been corrupted by a taste of lethal power. Without discipline and control imposed by fear or faith, these gunmen found unsavory satisfaction in murder rationalized, if at all, as revolution. Both organizations indicate the dangers when disputes about the legitimacy of the state opens opportunities for those who in stable societies would be either quiescent or a matter for the police. On the other hand both the Officials and the Provos—and in their original manifestation the INLA-IRSP—had a legitimacy derived from historical experience and contemporary roles, denied as always by the centers in

Belfast, Dublin and London but real enough in practice.

Essentially, the Officials did not want this heritage, did not after 1969 want to be a "movement" dominated by a secret army. Their secret IRA grew more secret, less legitimate, less military, and after a generation a matter of police concern alone. This direction arose from lessons learned or parsed from the recent past, from example, from the pressure of the schism in the movement that became final in 1969 and very bitter by 1970. Thus the Dublin center, the GHQ, the party, grew less and less enthusiastic about a Northern campaign. Few leaders went North. Few cared to know about military opportunities. Because of distaste, control was lax. The local commanders in the North made the operational decisions based on chance, opportunity, and the limitations imposed from Dublin—no sectarian bombs, for example. This Dublin decision had limited ideological logic—bombs that created turmoil in the streets were sectarian but shooting a Protestant politician like John Taylor was not. What Dublin really wanted was an end to the "military" campaign to allow full concentrations on politics. So Dublin read all Northern events through glazed spectacles. The errors of the Northern militants were not written off but presented as reason to end all operations. The bomb at Aldershot that killed not soldiers but a priest and women cleaners indicated the dangers of a further military campaign. On March 24, the British government closed Stormont—the Orange System dismantled—and thus force from Dublin would no longer be crucial, no longer be needed. In May, the murder of Ranger William Best by the Derry IRA, one of the most effective Official units under John Whyte, a sound, disciplined group, the equal of the Provos under Martin McGuinness, hardened Dublin's regard. On May 29, an Official truce was announced that the leadership wanted to be both permanent and total.

Since violence was no longer needed for Dublin's aims, it was no longer a valid means to act on Irish events, except at the margins to raise money and for a time to calm the militants. Still this current away from the military that in retrospect appeared inevitable and irreversible was not so apparent to the involved at the time. Those like Mike Ryan in operations, Costello until 1974 and others at GHQ assumed that the military was still important. Increasingly for Garland and Goulding it was no longer *very* important. The shift away from the military had a profound effect on Official IRA targeting: control remained at the local level and the only real GHQ contribution was criticism for error and caution as reward. Almost all the highly controversial operations—the murder by mistake of Senator Jack Barnswell, on December 12, 1971, the attempt on John Taylor, the death of Ranger Best—were carried out on local initiative. Aldershot had been planned for some time before Bloody Sunday and was managed from England. The militants within the movement like Seamus Costello, who was expelled, and Ryan, who was not, had less scope as politics absorbed everyones time, the movements resources, and attention. There was in effect very little control and few commands from the center. Every event, each target taught Dublin the lesson that had already been learned: a military campaign was ideologically unsound, personally unpleasant, and best ended as soon as possible—lessons that arose not from events but from the political and psychological needs of the leadership.

The Provos provided a quite different picture. They felt that their movement was the legitimate heir to centuries of revolutionary Republicanism and they were emboldened by this belief, held even by many of their most deadly foes in Ireland. They wanted a war, planned for a war, and by 1971, with considerable help from their enemies, had a war. For military purposes their IRA center chose targets or tolerated local choice for a generation through various regimes that, despite a stable formal structure and despite a relatively constant leadership group, embodied various styles and approaches.

The problem with revolutionary control at the margins of an armed struggle is that there is never a satisfactory solution: the nifty mix of flexibility and discipline cannot be institutionalized, cannot be adjusted day by day because of communications problems, cannot in fact ever be assured. The very small groups, Saor Éire and the INLA, had no margins and the Officials effectively chose not to have a center; but the Provos had grown grand by 1971 and remained large even when the number of active service volunteers declined under pressure after the 1975 truce period. The IRA was, relatively speaking, huge for an active underground. In the year April 1973 to April 1974, for example, 1,292 "terrorists"—mostly Republicans—were charged with criminal offences of a serious nature. Thus, for twenty years, control from the IRA center has varied from too loose—the nature of the leaders, the incompetence of those involved, the pressure on communication—to fairly firm—the strength of the leadership, the reduction in the number of operations, the demands for careful pre-planning beyond reliance on the locals, to keep up the pressure. Thus MacStiofáin by his nature ran a firm, at times almost one-man, show out of the center, but as the campaign escalated, an enormous number of targeting decisions was made locally. In contrast Eamon O'Doherty as Chief of Staff was less interested in administration and control and more concerned with overseeing specific operations. Once again there was much local control. This was often true when a new C/S moved in but more so when the center not only permitted but urged local initiative, as did Seamus Twomey. As British pressure grew more effective, Gerry Adams, Martin McGuinness and Ivor Bell exerted more control but not at risk of schism. After 1986

---

[1] Even by the summer of 1990 the future of Republican Sinn Fein was still uncertain. They had the sympathy of the traditionalists and many of the active service units habitually suspicious of the city—Belfast for this campaign—and the evidence of a military campaign going poorly. Many feared the Provo center intended a political direction—many physical force people always feared this, at times justifiably. On the other hand the IRA was better armed, courtesy of Libya than ever before, the IRA structure had stayed loyal including many traditionalists, and the center still controlled the money necessary to maintain the system and the armed struggle. RSF efforts to take over the NORAID base in America in 1989 might be considered a flanking maneuver to indicate that the money would exist to support dependents if the split widened. As a result the IRA Army Council was very careful in imposing orders in the countryside, wanting to offer no opportunity for disagreement. The result operationally was not always felicitous but independent blunders at the edges were hardly a novel experience for the center.

Republican Sinn Féin was a factor.[1]

The center could not risk exerting too much restraint. Always the margins had more freedom and thus made more "mistakes" than the center would have preferred. Some units historically did not accept guidance enthusiastically and the center was well aware of the dangers that might arise from local dissent in South Armagh or mid-Tyrone where there was a deep and abiding suspicion of the outside, the urban, the center.

The IRA Center

The nature of the IRA center meant that at times targeting ideas started from the core (the attempt on General Freeland), or from the Army Council (the post-truce Belfast bomb blitz). Almost always these core decision are obvious to the entire movement: British generals are patent targets, a bomb blitz was needed to reveal to the British the cost of staying and not negotiating. Thus sniping in Derry, bombs in cars, country ambushes can be stopped or escalated from the center but are usually a local matter. There have been tens of thousands of completed operations and very few began at the center. When an operation is spectacular, the assassination of Ewart-Biggs or the Great Train robbery, the GHQ staff may not only authorize the operation but also insert a special team. Most operations that do come to the attention of the center arise from local intelligence and movement needs: the first bombs in England in 1973 were suggested by a Belfast staff officer Jimmy Brown, pushed by the Belfast Brigade up to MacStiofáin who was not enthusiastic about bombing in Britain, and then carried out, ineptly, by a Belfast team during a time when the center was unmanned—MacStiofáin in prison, Joe Cahill in Libya, and J.B. O'Hagan holding the fort as Acting C/S. The operation, however, was an obvious ploy and had in various guises been discussed for a long while. The bombs came as no surprise to any of those involved—including the British Special Branch who had picked up informer rumours that in turn sharped their response to an on-going possibility. So most decisions are made and carried out at the edges unless they are novel or have policy implications—and even then the margin has been known to go ahead without informing GHQ or Northern Command. There is usually a mix of vulnerability discovered, IRA capacity, degree of risk, and policy needs. After Bobby Sands's death on hunger strike, there was a general IRA desire for revenge, for revenge in particular on Margaret Thatcher. What occurred was the discovery that the prime minister would be in a specific place (Brighton) at a specific time—the IRA intelligence officer even thought he had her location down to a particular room. This information was of no value if an attempt had to be made at that particular moment since security would be too tight. For some while, however, the IRA had possessed the technological capacity to construct a bomb that could be detonated weeks or even months after placement. This meant that an explosive device could be planted where Thatcher would be, long before there was a security cordon. And the bomb could then be detonated at the appropriate time. Obviously the Army Council authorized the attempt just as they had discussed the prospects of effectively targeting the prime minister before the Brighton opportunity arose.

Target selection, then, is usually a mix of local intelligence discovering a vulnerability (for local reasons, by luck, by intention, or on orders from the center) and pursuing the operation without recourse to the center. The further the operation is from the center in time of communication, the more likely the locals will act independently. Sometimes when there *is* authorization the actual operation occurs months later in quite a different context and often with less than felicitous results, as the Officials discovered with Aldershot. Academics and analysts are too prone to assume tight control with, as a result, detailed rationales for operations that in truth were prepared long before in quite different conditions. Sometimes, of course, the lead time is short, as with the Belfast bomb blitz—the resources were to hand at the same time as the need for a display arose—or the motive obvious, as with the bomb at Brighton. Thatcher was obviously on any IRA target list even before the hunger strikes and even ex-prime ministers are at risk.

In sum, the IRA center (the C/S, the GHQ, the Northern Command or the Army Council, the one man or several men who run the campaign) rarely fine-tunes target selection, mostly enthusiastically accepts or authorizes local initiative and thus finds it difficult to criticize when such initiative proves inept or counterproductive. What advice can be offered: avoid mistakes; think; be careful? There is very little the center can do in the short run—and the IRA is managed in the short run for long-term purposes, given the quality of talent available.

Sensible commanders would not put so many civilians at risk, would not always assume that errors will cancel out, would foresee confusions and blunder. Sensible commanders, however, would probably not undertake a revolutionary campaign with such talents, such scanty resources, with so great a dependence on history and the will of the Irish people, with such criminal optimism.

All revolutionary organizations are thus inherently inefficient, have very serious operational problems; but waiting for brilliant commanders, the proper equipment, and the ideal, absolutely vulnerable target to appear will win no wars. Thus the IRA center, by nature, by habit and by experience must let the margins take such risks so that persistence is guaranteed, so that escalation may occur, so that enthusiasm to act is not lost, so that schism is not risked, so that the war can be waged. The center can and does seek particular opportunities by asking local intelligence about vulnerabilities that will have major tactical, even strategic importance. The center can and usually does greet operational suggestion with enthusiasm, but not always. Some targets are eschewed, some goals and means are considered stunts or proven failures from past experience, some are simply too alien, too complex, too demanding, and others come to the center under the wrong auspices. The IRA, then, dominated by long experience and a generation of practice, currently engaged in a protracted campaign to erode the British will, largely moves ahead without great guidance. Just to maintain present momentum absorbs most efforts and nearly all of the center's time and interest.

The pattern of targets selected indicates that there are a few most desired targets: the military and the élite leadership. These are the same targets most regular armies would seek and the IRA aspires to be a real if not a regular army. Because the struggle is political and a matter of perception, the symbolic and political targets play a greater part in the campaign than they would in a real war where assassination, given all, is a rare recourse of the embattled leadership. Also among the hard, unpleasant targets are heretics and informers, who are more dangerous than the uniformed enemy. As the desirable military-élite targets are hardened, then the IRA moves out to softer but similar targets: the RUC reserve instead of the British army or the British army in Germany instead of the British army in Belfast. Then secondary targets are chosen: bureaucrats or construction workers or associates of the guilty. And finally and with reluctance for ideological and practical reasons, civilians who are representative of broad enemy groups—Protestants, English civilians, or diners at five-star restaurants. These are the target categories of terrorists whose most extreme members believe no one is innocent. In contrast, the IRA defenders would point to civilians killed intentionally by the RAF in a strategic bombing campaign directed at whole cities. And competence can be found; for with Martin McGuinness as O/C, the IRA bombed away the commercial center of Derry without harming any civilians. Derry's example has been obscured by notorious disasters, like the civilians, women, tourists, children, gunned down in Europe, or like Enniskillen, La Mon, Claudy: targets locally chosen and ineptly bombed with horrific results for the innocent and for the IRA's image. IRA targeting is involved in several processes: moving from hard targets to soft, moving up technologically so that this process can be reversed, moving up and down in intensity according to capacity, opportunity, and policy, moving both as in the past and, largely as a result of individual personal initiative, in novel directions. What the IRA would like is to have the capacity to strike at the core of the British military-government establishment without endangering civilians, without excessive risk to their own, with the assurance that such operations will shorten the protracted conflict, even end the long war. What the IRA can do is persist, a secret army, burden by history, by inherent incompetence and by limited material and personal resources, occasionally escalating the conflict but also sometimes losing momentum. Increasingly, then, what they can *not* do is offer much in the way of target-surprise. Even new techniques, new technological assets, new talents that permit "new" targets will arise from historical example. The IRA plays by history's rules, targets as history dictates.

In Sum

The selection process is not institutionalized. Suggestion arises most often around vulnerabilities, such as the routine of the Northern Ireland minister, usually spotted in conventional categories by local volunteers or friends. Some target choices arise from the ideas of volunteers, ideas that fit the rules, are conventional. The IRA is relatively conservative, suspicious of stunts, complexity and the investment of great resources. And the IRA has limited technological skills although over the years it has managed to cope and even to make use of the most sophisticated means for a variety of purposes, from monitoring British communication to thwarting anti-insurgency devices. Thus few IRA targets, no matter how deceptive the actual operation, offer surprise. Not only are most targets locally chosen to follow the rules of play but also most operations are undertaken without recourse to authorization. Sometimes the regional HQ staff may be aware of the intentions but sometimes not. At bottom the man with the gun does the deciding, while only rarely, very rarely indeed, does the center of the IRA circle become involved beyond simply authorization. Can Thatcher be targeted? If so then let the attempt be directed by those on the scene with the proper skills.

In most operations command is local. A few operations from the first London bomb blitz in 1973 or the attack on Ambassador Ewart-Biggs had special teams designated because the targets fell outside local competence. The various continental operations are handled by special units sent out by GHQ with, at first, limited local contacts. European control passes increasingly over to the locals. Command at the top usually ends with the selections of a prime symbolic target or with advice on focusing on a category of targets or at most on increasing or decreasing the intensity level. Control, then, increases as one goes down the ladder of command so that local command and volunteers always play a major role; this is particularly true when communication is difficult. Then, out of touch but in tune with practice, the margins operate independently and always with a time lag, focus on a target approved in the past under different conditions. The London bomb blitz in 1973, timed to steal attention from the border plebiscsite on the same day, was a rare operationally effective action at a distance—if at some volunteer cost.

When analysed the actual operations are dramatic but unrevealing in most cases. Sometimes they reflect the dynamics of the movement (Costello's assassination) but they rarely determine future directions. (With or without the death of Ranger Best in Derry in May 1972 the Official IRA was going to be largely disbanded by the center). The *lessons learned* in matters of targeting are those the movement wants to learn. The Provos are aware that punishing enthusiasm, no matter how misguided and counterproductive to movement aims, leads to schism or to dissent. Certain targets can be denied to the volunteers and certain efficiencies advocated, but the IRA center must make do with existing assets, with cultural limitation quite beyond control or even in some cases recognition. History not only rules but rules out many options beyond capacity no matter how obvious the lessons from the arena.

So at the end IRA strategy comes down to tactics, targeting the vulnerable, persisting, escalating if possible, always willing to suffer more for the Republic. In the fullness of time, the long war, the armed struggle will break the will of the British—so history rules. The IRA has tactics as strategy and history as example.

The Sources

Essentially the sources for the text are the thousands of hours of discussions, formal and informal, with those involved. These interviews, seldom narrowly focused on targets or tactics, have been buttressed by the conventional printed matter ranging from Republican publications through the distilled analysis and reports of scholars. Even a skimpy bibliography would exclude some of the useful publications but there have been three books solely on the IRA, my own *Secret Army* (republished in Dublin by Poolbeg in 1989), Tim Pat Coogan's *The IRA* (regularly republished and currently in Fontana paperback), and the newer *The Provisional IRA* (London: Heinemann, 1987) by Patrick Bishop and Eamonn Mallie, now also available in paperback.

THE SECRET ARMY
The IRA
1916-1979

J. Bowyer Bell

The definitive work on the IRA

POOLBEG